Every Woman's Journey

ೲ

Answering "Who Am I?" For the Feminine Heart

By Katrina J. Zeno
www.wttm.org

In memory of
Pope John Paul II,
my spiritual father,
who showed the world
how to make
a sincere gift of self.

Published by Women of the Third Millennium
P.O. Box 23673
Tempe, AZ 85285
480-720-5715
www.wttm.org
Comments may be sent to Katrina@wttm.org.

All Scripture quotations are taken from the New
American Bible, Confraternity of Christian Doctrine
(New York: Thomas Nelson Publishers, 1970)
unless otherwise footnoted.

ISBN 0-9748288-0-7
Library of Congress Control Number 2005902897

Cover design and layout by Beth Hart.

ಬಿ *Table of Contents* ಬಿ

Introduction..1

Chapter 1
First a Daughter, Then a Bride 3

Chapter 2
Why Male and Female? 17

Chapter 3
The Genius of Women 29

Chapter 4
Sin and the Nuptial Meaning of the Body 41

Chapter 5
Weaving a Tapestry of Life 61

Chapter 6
The Spouse of the Spirit............................ 79

Chapter 7
What About the Men? 105

Chapter 8
Women Priests: Why Not? 123

Chapter 9
Women in the Third Millennium:
Our Dignity, Vocation, and Mission 131

Post-Script 143

Introduction

ഇ

_I_ t was an unlikely place for a confession. With adding machines on one side and file folders on the other, the attractive woman in her mid-thirties didn't care about the Office Max surroundings. The cry of her heart was too insistent to be stifled.

"Katrina, I don't know who I am," she blurted out. "I know it sounds crazy, but that's the way I feel."

No, it didn't sound crazy. I'd heard the same confession from women over Chinese food, on the phone, and while having coffee. Widows who felt dismissed from life, mothers who'd packed their last child off to college, and single professional women hemmed in by the dull routine of everyday life had all breached the same question: "Who am I?"

It sounds trite, almost childish to verbalize it. After all, women tell themselves, "I'm a mother." "I'm an accountant." "I'm a wife." "I'm a religious sister." "Of course I know who I am..." And yet, we don't.

Tucked away in the recesses of every woman's heart is a longing for more. "Am I only a mother? Only a wife? Only a teacher or nurse? If I'm not only these things, then who am I?"

Digging into a woman's heart and soul for her deepest sense of identity isn't a one-time event. It's a journey. Women keep asking, "Who am I?" at different stages in life because a woman's identity isn't stagnant like a self-contained brackish pond. Her identity pushes on like a bold river, rushing around the next bend, carving a deeper, wider path.

If you've ever found yourself asking, "Who am I?" then I invite you to jump in. The current might feel a bit cold and scary at first, but once you learn to befriend the rushing river and flowing current, you'll go places you never imagined possible. And best of all, you'll learn to love the journey.

Chapter 1

ℬ⊃⪼

First a Daughter, Then a Bride

*L*ife was supposed to be oh, so simple: I'd grow up, get married, have a family, enjoy my grandchildren, sit in the sun during retirement, and die at a happy old age. But that's not what happened.

Somewhere along the line, the Author forgot the story line. It changed. I changed. My whole world changed. I had to search for a new identity, a new understanding of God, and a new mission. Instead of getting the life I signed up for, I had to discover the one God designed for me from all eternity.

My life had all the makings of *Fortune 500* success. I was born and raised in San Diego, California, when it was a sleepy big city. Living one mile from the beach, perched on a mountain that connected the middle-class suburb of Pacific Beach to the ritzy suburb of La Jolla, I could walk to public grade school and then later bike to my high school on Mission Bay.

As a teenager, I thought nothing of taking the bus by myself to downtown San Diego for gymnastics or of playing hide-and-seek with my theater friends in the world-famous San Diego Zoo. Life was safe, secure, and comfortable.

Ditto for home. As the fifth of six children in a wonderful Catholic family, I thought everyone grew up with their father emptying the dishwasher, taking the family camping for vacation, having meals together, and playing "spoons" until midnight on New Year's Eve.

My Catholic upbringing was especially rich. My mother was way ahead of her time. Or should I say Mary Reed Newland,[1] whom my mother read and imitated, was way ahead of her time. There was no need for Santa Claus in our home. St. Nick and his feastday on December 6 were festively celebrated. Lent meant getting a purple bean for each sacrifice made and praying the Stations of the Cross with 14 candles.

Holy Thursday found us gathered around the Passover table where the menu included bitter herbs (from the dandelions in our front lawn) and red bricks made from Jello. We spent Good Friday in quiet from noon until 3 p.m., with the phone off the hook and a "do not disturb" sign on the front door. Baptismal days, feast days, Advent, and Pentecost were all celebrated in creative, tangible ways.

Getting to Know Him

Even with this rich upbringing, I lacked one thing. I knew a lot about Jesus, but I didn't know Jesus personally. It would be as if I told you about my best friend Maureen. Maureen has red hair, freckles, played the trombone in high school, and is easygoing. However, you wouldn't know her personally until I actually introduced you to her face-to-face. It was the same with Jesus. I knew a lot about him, but I didn't know him personally.

All that changed at 16. While most of my peers were rejecting religion, I attended a Youth Encounter Retreat weekend. There I noticed these people had something I didn't have. I didn't know what it was, but I was curious. As the retreat progressed, I heard for the first time that I could give my life to Jesus and know him personally as a close friend.

I took the plunge. On Sunday of the retreat, I asked my small group to pray for me to give my life to Jesus. As they prayed, I cried. As they continued to pray, I continued to cry. When they stopped praying, I was still crying. I felt as if Mount Olympus had been lifted from my shoulders even though I didn't know why I was crying.

Of course, I realize now God was answering my prayer. He was helping me release my life to him and all the pent up hurts and anxieties that went with it. Jesus was no longer someone "out there." He was now close and personal. I'd met God face-to-face, or more accurately, heart-to-heart.

No Mid-Life Crisis

That was truly the beginning of a new life for me, although there wasn't a dramatic external change. I was a straight A student, I never smoked or drank, and I obeyed my parents. However, an interior change began to take place. God had taken the central place in my life. Jesus was becoming my best friend, and I started reading the Bible to get to know God better.

In the brashness of my late teens I can remember thinking I was never going to go through mid-life crisis. I knew my identity was in God and that was that. It would carry me through to my grave.

I was wrong.

Over the past 25 years, and especially the past 15, I have asked myself many, many times: "Who am I?" It's amazing how many times in life we revisit this question. It's like a pesky fly that won't go away. You bat at it, and it goes away for a while, but it returns again and again. Finally, out of desperation, you get a fly swatter and smack, victory at last! But it's only for a little while, until you hear bzzz, bzzz...and the cycle starts all over again.

How do we deal with this pesky fly that won't leave us alone? Is it possible to answer the question "Who am I?" once and for all?

I thought I had the answer down pat: At 16, I had given my life to Christ and made him the focus of my identity. At 18, I graduated as valedictorian of my high school with a 4.00 GPA. At 19, I married my high school sweetheart, and at 20, I left San Diego to study theology at Franciscan University of Steubenville in Ohio. (Yes, you read it right. I left San Diego for *Ohio*.)

In Ohio, we had a couple rough transition years, but we managed. We became part of a dynamic Catholic community of families. I graduated third in my college class and received the senior theology award. My husband opened his own business. I worked for a pro-life organization for a year, and then our wonderful son Michael was born.

Seamless Garment

I had the life I signed up for—a good husband, a healthy son, Christian fellowship, intellectual stimulation, supportive relationships, and a home in a nice neighborhood. My life was like a seamless garment. Everything was neatly connected: my social life, spiritual life, part-time work, and intellectual life all evolved around the same Catholic community.

Then the garment began to unravel. For many years my husband had struggled with his personal identity. God intervened at certain crisis points and the issue would go underground for a while, but it would always pop up again. I'd run out of strategies. We'd moved, we'd joined a Catholic community, and we'd started our family, but the issue kept resurfacing.

In the Pit

When our son Michael was almost three, we agreed on a temporary separation with the intention of getting back together. Over the next year, I went through one of the darkest periods in my life. My mind was so saturated with pain I couldn't think of praying in a conversational way. I turned to rote prayers to give me words to say. I beseeched the heavens for help and discovered Mary as my mother and the saints as my friends.

During this time, my friends often exhorted me to call them when I was feeling down. I quickly realized this was impossible. I couldn't pick up the phone and say, "Hi, this is Katrina. I just called to tell you I'm feeling numb and depressed and I'm not even sure I'm going to make it."

I couldn't do it. I needed them to call me. So I asked five women in my faith sharing group to take a day of the week and call me. With their help, I made it through the worst month of my life and started inching toward the top of the pit.

Then God broke through my darkness.

Learning Through Contrast

One night at a women's prayer meeting, I felt suddenly bathed in a shaft of light. I stood there soaking in the light because up to that point, I hadn't realized how dark the darkness had been.

In that moment, God showed me the value of contrast. Just as parents teach their children right/left, up/down, in/out, stop/go, so, too, the Lord teaches us through contrast. He teaches us through light and darkness, fullness and aridity, joy and sorrow, intimacy and abandonment. I was so thankful the light had come and pierced my darkness, even though it didn't remove all the pain.

What was the source of my pain? It was the pain of a crushed identity. My whole life I had lived and breathed marriage as a sacrament, as a reflection of Christ's unbreakable bond of love for the Church. And now I was no longer that reflection. With my marriage failing, I felt as if someone had taken my identity, placed it on a table and smashed it into a million pieces. The seamless garment wasn't just unraveling; it was being ripped in two.

First a Daughter, Then a Bride!

But the Lord taught me something on my thirtieth birthday that year that completely changed my life. In prayer, he told me I was first a daughter, then a bride.

First a daughter, then a bride! Somewhere along the way in trying to figure out my identity as a woman, I'd forgotten the most fundamental truth of my life that before being a wife, mother, friend, teacher, or student, I was first a daughter of God.

God, in his mercy, ripped out the faulty foundation of straw and hay that he knew wouldn't last and was laying a new one of gold and precious stones.

I even stumbled on a Scripture that aptly described my situation. It's Isaiah 54:5-8:

> "For he who has become your husband is your Maker; his name is the Lord of hosts; Your redeemer is the Holy One of Israel, called God of all the earth.

> The Lord calls you back, like a wife forsaken and grieved in spirit, A wife married in youth and then cast off, says your God. For a brief moment I abandoned you, but with great tenderness I will take you back. In an outburst of wrath, for a moment I hid my face from you; But with enduring love I take pity on you, says the Lord, your redeemer."

Since my thirtieth birthday I have never been the same. Certainly, I've had to revisit many issues I thought were closed: Should I marry? Should I stay single? Should I work? How much should I work? Should I stay in Steubenville? Should I move back to San Diego? But the one question I've never asked myself again is who I am in the eyes of God, because I know that I am first a daughter, then a bride.

The Starting Point

For every woman, this is the starting point of the journey: to know she is a daughter of God before anything else. This is the rock-solid foundation that no amount of rain, wind, disaster, or pain can destroy.

Why is this so important? Because knowing the Father's love is the heart of the gospel message. Jesus came to reveal God not as Judge or Lawgiver but as "Abba," "Father." When the disciples asked Jesus to teach them to pray, he began: "Abba, who art in heaven..." In Romans 8:15, St. Paul pens the perfect roadside billboard to announce the Fatherhood of God: "You did not receive a spirit of slavery leading you back into fear, but a spirit of adoption through which we cry out, 'Abba!' (that is 'Father')."

Dismissing Fatherhood

The tragedy of modern culture is its attempt to remove the billboard, to wipe out the Fatherhood of God. Nothing could be more harmful to the journey, to discovering our identity as women. If God isn't our Father, then we aren't his daughters. And if we aren't his daughters, then we are orphans. We're alone and destitute, with no one to help us.

A friend of mine once described her fear of being an orphan in this way: She saw herself as a little girl running down the sidewalk, when suddenly she fell flat on her face. Her automatic response was to stuff away the pain, scrape herself off the sidewalk, and keep going.

One day, in prayer, she felt the Lord telling her to remain on the sidewalk, face down waiting. She was petrified! She was scared no one would come to help her. She was afraid God would leave her there as an orphan.

God the Father did come to help, and it was one of the biggest breakthroughs in her spiritual life. She finally realized she didn't have to do it on her own. She experienced God as Father and herself as a beloved daughter.

This attack on the Fatherhood of God doesn't originate with modern culture. It's Satan's strategy from the beginning. Ever since Adam and Eve, he's been trying to convince us we're orphans, that we don't have a loving Father, and we'll be left face down on the sidewalk having to fend for ourselves. Satan is the father of lies, and this is his most destructive one because it goes to the core of our identity.

The best way to combat a lie is to replace it with truth. 1 John 3:1 tells us the truth of our relationship with God: "See what love the Father has bestowed on us in letting us be called children of God! Yet that is what we are."

God With Us

In the Gospel of John, Jesus constantly talks about his relationship with the Father. "The Father and I are one" (Jn. 10:30). "Now I am leaving the world to go to the Father" (Jn. 16:28). And my favorite verse: "Yet, I can never be alone; the Father is with me" (Jn. 16:32).

We are never alone. The Father is with us. The Father is with you even when you feel alone, isolated, flat on the pavement of life. The truth is **the Father is always with you.**

Jesus told a beautiful parable about our relationship with God the Father and how each of our lives is like a pilgrimage to the Father's house. It's the parable of the prodigal son in Luke 15.

Prodigal Son Revisited

I thought nothing more could be said about this parable until I attended a conference in Walsingham, England, in the summer of 2000. There, Bishop Joseph Ekuwen of Nigeria said the parable of the prodigal son tells each of our stories because it tells the universal story of mankind.

Here's how he described it: At one point in time (before original sin), we lived in harmony with the Father (God) and the elder brother (others). We lived in the Father's house. Then, through our offense (original sin) we broke our relationship with the Father and went our own way.

However, despite our unfaithfulness, God has always been faithful. He constantly watches for us, expecting our return. When we return, the Father not only forgives us, but reconciles us to the family. This is the symbolism of the ring, robe, sandals, and festive celebration—it means the Father welcomes us back into the life of the family. He restores us to the same relationship we had with him before any offense.

More Than Forgiveness

Here's the point Bishop Ekuwen made: God the Father goes beyond forgiveness to reconciliation. The Father doesn't just forgive us and keep us at an arm's distance. He welcomes us back into the family. **He restores us to the same relationship we had with him before any offense.**

The elder brother goes ballistic. He's furious that his irresponsible, younger brother is brought back into the family with the same status and privileges.

But notice what the father says to the elder brother: "You are with me always." Frequently, this sentence slips by us, but it's the most important thing the father could have said! He's reminding the elder son (and us) that **the essence of fatherhood is not provision, but presence.** His fatherhood impelled him to welcome back his child not as a slave, but as a son, so he could be in the father's presence.

To the Father's House

This is where we need to find ourselves—in the Father's presence, in the Father's house. Not only have we been forgiven by the death of Jesus Christ, but we've been reconciled to God the Father. God welcomes us back not as a slave, but as a beloved daughter. Jesus Christ restores our relationship with God as it was before any offense.

Take a moment and ask yourself: Do I experience my life as a journey to the house of the Father, a Father whose unconditional love has melted my heart so that I know I am his daughter?

Or am I struggling with my foundational identity, with my self worth? Do I draw the majority of my identity from mothering, from how well my children act at a restaurant, in Church, at school, or when company comes over? Am I afraid others think poorly of me because of choices I make, or my husband makes, or because of family struggles with alcohol or addiction? Do I try to validate and prove my worth through my work, looks, or sexual relations?

Perhaps you're not married, but single, and you feel you've been forgotten and ignored, that you're missing out on life because you're not a bride. Or maybe you're a widow or divorced and you've been through the same wrenching I have and you're not quite sure where to turn to re-root your identity. Or maybe you've been hurt, abandoned, or abused by your earthly father or another man and the thought of a heavenly Father is not consoling but frightening or repulsive.

For all these reasons and more, it can be difficult for us to relate to God as Father, to know our foundational identity as a daughter.

We must beg God to bring us into his presence, to remove the faulty foundation of straw and hay in our lives and replace it with the one that will last forever.

Entering the Father's Presence

I invite you to take 15 minutes in a quiet place and read the following meditation. I hope it will help you rediscover your identity as a daughter and begin the journey anew in the Father's presence.

> Imagine yourself in the home you grew up in as a little girl. Look around, smell the familiar smells. See yourself sitting in the living room or family room

and your father comes walking into the room (even if you never knew him). He stops, sees you, and walks over to you. He sits down opposite you, looks you in the eyes and says to you, "How do you feel about me?"

You hesitate, not quite sure what to say, but then he says it again: "Really, how do you feel about me?" With that permission, you let the dam break and all your hidden thoughts, pains, and fears come flooding out. What do you say to your father?

Now hear your father say back to you: "Is there anything else?" and you feel rise up within you the one thing you've always wanted to say to your father, but were afraid. What is it? What do you want to say? You can say it to him now. It's safe. Tell him.

And now your father takes both your hands and looks again into your eyes and says to you, "Tell me, my daughter, how have I failed you?" You look back at him, and the little girl inside you says: "Dad, you failed me when..." What do you say to him?

After telling your dad the things that hurt you, see him reach out and gather you into his arms and hold you close to his heart and say to you, "I'm sorry, I'm so sorry, my daughter. I had no idea how much I hurt you. If I had known, I never would have done that. I'm sorry, so, so sorry."

Now imagine yourself as that same girl in heaven. See yourself approaching the throne of God the Father. As you approach, the Father gets up and walks to meet you. He takes you by the hand and you walk up to the throne hand in hand, only you don't go up to the throne. Instead, you stop at the steps, and he sits down on the steps and invites you to sit beside him.

See the Father look at you and say, "Tell me, my daughter, how do you feel about me?" You hesitate, afraid to tell the King of the Universe what you really feel, but then he says, "It's all right. Tell me how you feel about me." What do you say to him? Hear yourself tell God the Father how you feel about him.

Now see God the Father take both your hands, bring you around in front of him, put you on his lap and say to you tenderly: "Now tell me, how do you feel I have failed you?" It's safe. You're in the Father's house, you can tell him anything. There's nothing to hide. Tell the Father how you feel he has failed you.

Now hear the Father say, "Is there anything else you want to tell me?" What do you say to him? Pour your heart out to him.

When you're done, see the Father stand up, pick you up, and enfold you in his arms. Feel the warmth of the universe surround you and hear him say in your ear: "I'm sorry. I'm so, so sorry, my daughter, for all the pain and suffering you endured."

ಬಂಡ

Questions for Reflection and Discussion

1. How would you describe your relationship with God right now?

2. Have you ever thought of yourself as a daughter of God? If this isn't your foundational identity, what is?

3. What prevents you from drawing closer to God as Father?

4. Take a moment and write a letter to God starting with "Dear Father." Write whatever comes to mind without censoring it.

Chapter 2

ഇൻൽ

Why Male and Female?

Refounding my identity as a daughter of the Father was only the first chapter in re-creating my feminine soul. As the years passed, I discovered there was more.

Lady in Waiting

After the annulment of my marriage, I assumed I would remarry. I assumed I just had to maintain my little, part-time job until Prince Charming came along and rescued me.

There's a name for this mentality. It's called a "lady-in-waiting," and I was guilty of it. I was waiting for a man to come and rescue me from the circumstances I hadn't chosen. I was waiting for a new romantic relationship to bring sparks and energy and purpose into my life. I was waiting...waiting...waiting....

After a couple of years of waiting, I realized I was like a stalled car—all the potential to accelerate was there, but I wasn't moving. I had to jettison the marriage assumption and learn to walk in the weightlessness of single life. I had to decide what I wanted to *do* for the rest of my life to earn a living. **I had to learn what it meant to be a woman without a man.**

Swirling around me was a smorgasbord of opinions. Books, talk-show hosts, and educational experts advised me to throw off the shackles of gender roles and remake myself as an autonomous "womyn," without reference to a man. But I wanted truth, not opinion. And I found that truth in the writings of Pope John Paul II.

John Paul II's teachings on women are innovative and timeless. He unveiled the deepest cry of a woman's heart with the tenderness and love of a bridegroom lifting the veil on his bride. Unfortunately, the media didn't usually portray him this way. More often they presented a cranky, old celibate in Rome who wanted to keep women "in their place." Nothing could have been further from the truth. John Paul II championed human dignity, and especially the beauty and dignity of women.

Same or Different?

In order to grasp the innovative nature of John Paul II's teachings, it's helpful to place him in context, to see him as a Rolls Royce at the end of a long and complicated assembly line of philosophers and theologians. Fortunately, we don't have to review the entire 2500-year history of thinking on women since Sister Prudence Allen, RSM, has done a remarkable job in her two-volume set, *The Concept of Woman*.[1] Instead, we can look at just two ancient philosophers, Plato and Aristotle, and two Christian theologians, Augustine and Aquinas.

Plato's writings about women are quite surprising. He maintained there was no fundamental difference between women and men. He thought the soul was the true nature of the person, and since the soul was neither male nor female, women and men were essentially the same. True to his own teaching, Plato included women in his inner circle of students.

Aristotle occupies the opposite end of the spectrum. He thought men were naturally superior to women. He described the male as active, fertile, rational, and made to rule, while the female was passive, infertile, irrational, and made to obey. In short, Aristotle defined woman as an imperfect man.

Still Uncertain

While we can be indignant at pagan philosophers' attempts to figure out the similarities and differences between men and women, Christian philosophers and theologians struggled with similar problems.

Following Plato's lead, Augustine said there was no difference between the soul of the male and female. However, in the physical world, he thought the female was less the image of God. Looking at her role as "helper," Augustine said the woman was more involved with the things of the earth, with the physical world, and this made her less spiritual and therefore less like God.

Good News

Finally, Thomas Aquinas heralds good news and bad news. The good news is men and women are made equally in the image of God because we both have an intelligent nature. For Aquinas, our ability to think rationally is how we reflect God most perfectly. Unlike the animals, human persons have an intellect and will. This allows us to image God through reason and free choice.

Bad News

Now for the bad news. Aquinas also thought the male contained the image of God more perfectly than the female. In his interpretation of Genesis 2, Aquinas said the male received an immediate transfer of the divine image because he was created directly by God. This immediate transfer is absent in the female's creation because she was derived from the male.

I think of this as his separate but equal clause: male and female are equal because they are both rational creatures, but there's a hierarchy of perfection in which the male more perfectly images God than the female.

I'm afraid if Aquinas or Aristotle were alive today they might be shredded to pieces, not just by radical feminists, but by any one who senses a devaluation of the feminine in favor of the masculine.

Mars...Venus...Earth?

As a result of this devaluation, our current age continues to be caught between two extremes. On the one hand, we have women arguing there are no real differences between male and female and so all differences should be wiped out. On the other swing of the pendulum, we have women saying the differences are fundamentally important and, in fact, women are superior to men.

This is where I found myself—smack in the midst of the gender battle. Are men and women the same or different? Is gender imposed on us by culture or is it part of our being? Are men from Mars and women from Venus...or from some other planet?

Fortunately, I didn't have to fight this battle on my own— John Paul II had entered the fray before me.

Something New!

John Paul II spent years studying and meditating on the nature of men and women while earning graduate degrees in philosophy and theology. As a parish priest, he counseled married couples and camped with them. As pope, he spent hours in prayer before the Eucharist and at the altar. The fruit of his life is a new synthesis within this age-old debate about men and women.

To dig out John Paul II's new synthesis, we have to go back to the first years of his pontificate. In September 1979, less than one year after his surprise election as pope, John Paul II began a series of teachings based on Genesis 1 and 2.

In these teachings, John Paul II systematically presented the meaning of male and female as made in the image and likeness of God. These teachings were originally published in a little book called "Original Unity of Man and Woman," but have been republished in a larger collection entitled *The Theology of the Body*.[2]

"Original Unity of Man and Woman" is like uranium—compact and dense. It contains the nucleus of John Paul II's teachings about the dignity of men and women. Through these teachings, John Paul II introduced new terms such as nuptial meaning of the body, original solitude, original nakedness, and *communio personarum*.

This is what makes John Paul II both difficult and rewarding to read. By creating new language, he attempted to capture spiritual realities in human words. It's as if John Paul II was looking through the microscope of faith and trying to describe dimensions of the human person previously hidden from sight.

Back to the Beginning

With John Paul II as our guide, let's look through the microscope of faith. Let's go back to "the beginning," back to Genesis 1 and 2 to take a new look at what Scriptures teaches us about the nature of men and women.

In Genesis 1:27 we read: "God created man in his image; in the divine image he created him; male and female he created them." This truth captivated John Paul II's life and thought. **Everything in *The Theology of the Body* attempts to understand how both male and female are made in the image and likeness of God.** And to penetrate the depth of this reality, John Paul II turned the microscope to Genesis 2 and the second account of creation.

In this account, male and female are not created at the same time. Instead, Genesis 2:7 tells us, "the Lord God formed man out of the clay of the ground and blew into his nostrils the breath of life, and so man became a living being."

Genesis 2:7 reveals something new about the human person: We are more than the material world, more than clay of the ground. We are also breath or spirit. (In Hebrew, the word for breath, *ruah*, also means spirit.)

Unique Creation

This is an important point. In all creation only human persons are this unique combination of matter and spirit. The animals aren't this combination because they're only matter. The angels aren't this unique combination because they're only spirit. Only human persons image God by being both body and spirit for, as John Paul II said, man "belongs to the visible world, but goes beyond it."[3]

Let's jump ahead a few verses to Genesis 2:18-20. In these verses, God decides to make a suitable partner for Adam, but none can be found. Adam is alone.

If we stop and think for a moment, we'll realize Adam really isn't alone. God, birds, cattle, and flowers fill this earthly paradise, and yet Adam experiences himself as alone. This is because no other creature is made in the image and likeness of God in the same way he is. Adam is alone because only Adam is both body and spirit.

No Longer Alone

How does God solve Adam's solitude? I have to admit, this is one of my favorite parts of Scripture. God casts Adam into a deep sleep, takes a rib from his side, and forms it into a woman. Upon waking from sleep and seeing the female, Adam gushes: "This one at last is bone of my bones and flesh of my flesh; This one shall be called 'woman' for out of 'man' this one has been taken" (Gen. 2:23).

Immediately, Adam recognizes (finally!! hallelujah!!)—here's another being who shares his same nature. Scripture could have said: "And God put Adam to sleep and fashioned another human being for him, ho hum...(yawn)," but it doesn't.

Showing Equality

As I learned in writing class, *show* don't *tell*. Scripture is *showing* us a fundamental truth: Men are not from Mars and women are not from Venus. **They're from the same body.** For John Paul II, this establishes the absolute equality of male and female. Men and women are equal because we come from the same body. We share the same nature.

Up to this point, Genesis 2 is carefully guiding us through a profound visual journey: 1) Adam is made of clay and breath (body and spirit); 2) Adam is alone; 3) Adam is still alone even after the creation of the animals; 4) God solves Adam's solitude by creating Eve from the side of Adam, from the same body.

Made for Communion

This creation journey is a carefully crafted symphony moving toward a crescendo, the crescendo of Genesis 2:24: "That is why a man leaves his father and mother and clings to his wife, and the two of them become one body." This is a crescendo of union. Yes, of marital union, but more fundamentally of interpersonal communion.

Genesis 2:24 is a crucial verse for John Paul II. It reveals the deepest essence of the human person. We are not made for solitude, but for communion. In fact, John Paul II proclaimed that "man becomes the image of God not so much in the moment of solitude as in the moment of communion."[4]

This is his new contribution to 2500 years of philosophy and theology—that the human person images God not only through his rationality, as Aquinas thought, but even more fundamentally through his ability for union and communion.[5]

A Tango Lesson

I love to dance Argentine tango, and there's a saying in tango most people know: it takes two to tango. The same is true of imaging God: it takes two to image God. If we only imaged God through our rationality, one would have been enough. Adam would have been sufficient.

But he wasn't. Just as it takes two to tango, it takes two to image God. Male and female image God *together*.

Now if you're not married, you're probably ready to chuck this book and think you've been left out again (!!@%##!). No, a thousand times no. Every person—young, old, single, married, with children, and without children—images God by living in interpersonal communion. Marriage is the original expression of this interpersonal communion, but it's not the only one (read on...).

The Spiral

One of the most difficult aspects of John Paul II's thinking and writing is his spiral style. Most novels, history books, and magazine articles are written in a linear way. They have a beginning, middle, and end that progress in a straightforward manner. But not John Paul II. He'll talk about something, go away from it for a while, and then revisit it on a deeper level. Instead of expecting John Paul II to always say something new, expect him to go deeper.

Becoming a Gift

We can see this spiral pattern in his writings on imaging God. Yes, we image God "not so much in the moment of solitude as in the moment of communion," but, as John Paul II wrote elsewhere, "To say that man [i.e., person] is created in the image and likeness of God means that man is called to exist 'for' others, to become a gift."[6] For John Paul II, the key word is "gift." **We image God by making a sincere gift of self.**

Why is this point stressed?

To answer that question we have to fast-forward to the New Testament and Jesus' revelation about the inner life of God. Jesus revealed that God was not only One, but Three. God is Trinity.

Unfortunately, the word "Trinity" often lacks visual content in our minds other than a triangle or St. Patrick's shamrock. When I think of God as Trinity, here's how I like to image it: **The Father pours himself out in gift to the Son. The Son pours himself out in gift to the Father, and the Holy Spirit bursts forth as the fruit of their self-giving love.**[7]

God is one nature, but in that one nature the Father and Son pour themselves out in gift to each other, and that gift is not sterile but fruitful. It bursts forth as the Holy Spirit.

Trinitarian Reflection

Here's the really cool part (forgive my youthful exuberance!). As human persons, we are one (human) nature, but we are also two—male and female—and so we can pour ourselves out in gift to each other. And that gift is meant to be fruitful.

God is a union and communion of fruitful, self-giving love. So, too, as human persons we are called to live in a union and communion of fruitful, self-giving love. If we live this way, others will be able to see God, the Trinity, through us and our self-giving.

God designed the family to be a human trinity in time and history. He designed the love of husband and wife to burst forth in the fruitfulness of children. But he also designed the love between parent and child, friend and friend, aunt and niece, and widow and grandchild to be spiritually fruitful (more about this in chapter 3).

The Divine Design

John Paul II loved to meditate on our ability to make a sincere gift of self, to self-donate. The male/female distinction is not culturally imposed or an evolutionary accident. It's the divine design. Male and female emerge from one human nature in order to pour themselves out in gift to each other, a gift that's designed to be fruitful, a gift that involves the whole person.

If we spiral back to the beginning of this chapter and ask again, "Are male and female the same or different?" the answer is "both." We're the same because we come from the same body and share the same nature, and we're different because we're male and female. Many of the male/female differences (both charming and maddening) have been catalogued by Dr. John Gray in his Mars and Venus books.[8] His insights have helped thousands of people understand why men and women think and act differently.

However, difference is only half the equation. Precisely because we're different *and the same* can we live in a union and communion of fruitful, self-giving love. Precisely because the Trinity is different *and the same* can the Trinity exist in a union and communion of fruitful, self-giving love.

Body Basics

I know these ideas are difficult and at times jolting because they're new and somewhat abstract. However, they're actually very concrete. Everything is based on the human body, on asking why God made us male and female, not male and male or female and female.

The reason is union. When we look at the male and female body, we can't help but notice that they go together, that they are made for union. This bodily reality opens our eyes to a spiritual reality—the reality that we are made for union and communion with God and others through a sincere gift of self.

Old Expressions Aren't Enough

John Paul II created a new expression to describe this interpersonal reality of union and communion. He called it the "nuptial (or spousal) meaning of the body." This was his innovative way of saying "The body is made for union."

The "body," however, refers to more than your physical body. It means your entire person. Your body expresses your person. It expresses who you are. Your entire being is made for spiritual, emotional, psychological, and interpersonal union.

One Way to Happiness

John Paul II considered the nuptial meaning of the body, *your* body, to be the fundamental element of existence in the world. In other words, if you don't realize you're made for union and communion through a sincere gift of self, you'll seek other sources of happiness. When this happens, our bodies are no longer the source of deeply personal and satisfying communion, but of frustration, hollowness, and pain (more about this in chapter 4).

Simplifying JP2

When my son was 10 years old, I tried to explain the nuptial meaning of the body to him at the dinner table. After seeing his puzzled expression (I can't imagine why), I devised a short-hand way of explaining it: **"We're made from one nature, embodied in two ways, for the purpose of union and communion through a sincere and fruitful gift of self."**

This description is worth committing to memory. It can change the whole way we view ourselves, others, and God. It can remind us constantly of how and why we were created as male and female: to be a gift. This truth defined John Paul II's life. As women on the journey, we're invited to do the same.

ℰↄℭ℞

Questions for Reflection and Discussion

1. What struck you about the views of Plato and Aristotle? What about Augustine and Aquinas?

2. Before this chapter, would you have said men and women are the same or different? Why?

3. What struck you in John Paul II's description of male and female as created from the same body? Does this change the way you view yourself and/or others?

4. Have you ever felt the loneliness Adam experienced where you couldn't "connect" with the world around you?

5. Do you agree or disagree with John Paul II's statement that the human person becomes the image of God "not so much in the moment of solitude as in the moment of communion"? Why?

6. Have you ever thought of yourself as a reflection of the fruitful, self-giving love of the Trinity?

7. Can you recall the description of the nuptial meaning of the body without looking at the previous page?

Chapter 3

ℰⱭℭℛ

The Genius of Women

ℰinstein was a genius. Beethoven was a genius. Michelangelo was a genius. Each of them had a unique ability to bring into being something that never existed before.

Women, too, have a creative genius. We have the unique ability to bring into being something that never existed before. To capture this unique ability, John Paul II coined a new term, the "genius of women." Rather than discounting women or recasting them in the image and likeness of men, John Paul II wanted to affirm the feminine way of doing things, to highlight the distinctive way a woman makes a gift of self.

The Real Meaning of 'Helper'

In speaking about the feminine genius, John Paul II broke new ground. While Augustine said woman's role as "helper" meant she was more bound up in the physical world, John Paul II's theology of the body takes a different route: Man, "after having become thoroughly aware of his own solitude among all living beings on earth, waited for 'a helper fit for him' (cf. Gen. 2:20). None of these beings (*anamalia*) offered man the basic conditions which make it possible to exist in a relationship of mutual giving."[1]

A bit later, he continues: "...'alone' man does not completely realize this essence [of being made in the image and likeness of God]. He realizes it only by existing 'with someone'—and even more deeply and completely—by existing 'for someone.'"[2]

The Gift of Woman

For John Paul II, being a "helper" doesn't refer to the practical things of life like cooking, cleaning, and caring for the kids. It means the woman helps the man discover his own humanity, his own capacity for relational self-giving.

Here's how I visualize it: Woman's first presence in the world was as gift. God created her and presented her as gift to man. By being gift to him, she showed him how to make a sincere gift of self. She revealed to him the nuptial meaning of his own body, that he was made for union and communion through a sincere gift of self.

The uniqueness of woman is awesome. Without her, the male cannot realize the meaning of his existence—to exist with and for someone. Nor can he understand fully what it means to be a person, to be created in the image and likeness of God for a sincere gift of self. Without her, the task of life is simply to care for the garden (i.e., to earn a living). But with her, man learns the meaning of life as union and communion through a sincere gift of self.

This explanation of the genius of women may work for the garden of Eden, but what about today? Am I suggesting women show up on the doorstep of eligible bachelors with a bow on their head and say, "I'm your gift!"? (Let me know if it works.)

The Empty Space

To help others understand the meaning of life as union and communion, God has given us a very concrete answer: the feminine body. The feminine body is radically different from the masculine body. For starters, we have curves, more connectors between the two sides of the brain, and less muscle mass. But there's another way the feminine body is different. Only women are created with an empty space within.

Women are created to be receptive, to be life-givers. A woman's entire being is oriented toward receiving and nurturing new life. We make a gift of self so that others can receive the gift of self, their very life.

Creative and Pro-Creative

The feminine genius indeed brings into being something that never existed before—a new human life. Far from being abstract and impersonal, the feminine gift of self is concrete, intimate, and highly personal. It involves the union of a woman's body with the child within.

In his apostolic letter, "On the Dignity and Vocation of Women," John Paul II reflected on this feminine gift of self: "Motherhood implies from the beginning [i.e., before original sin] a special openness to the new person.... In this openness...the woman discovers herself through a sincere gift of self." And in the next paragraph he adds: "Motherhood is linked to the personal structure of the woman and to the personal dimension of the gift."[3]

The very way a woman's being is knit together is for a sincere gift of self through motherhood. The feminine genius is meant to be creative and *pro*-creative.

Another Kind of Motherhood

But what about women who aren't mothers? Are they somehow excluded from the genius of women, from this feminine gift of self?

Not for a moment! Once again John Paul II spirals deeper by introducing another facet of a woman's being—that of spiritual motherhood. I like to think of the nature of woman as a sparkling diamond that John Paul II held up to the Light of faith. As he turned it this way and that, he admired the diamond and continued to describe the different ways it reflected the Light.

I might have been blind to this feminine facet of spiritual motherhood my whole life if it hadn't been for an unusual romantic relationship.

Bearing Christ to the World

A number of years ago, I began dating someone whose spirituality was from Eastern mysticism. For four months, God put me through a crash course in ecumenism and evangelization. As we explored our different spiritualities, I had to articulate what I believed about the cross, self-sacrificial love, redemption, and birth control.

In the process, I realized that while my explanations about the faith could till the soil of my friend's heart, ultimately he needed to experience the person of Jesus Christ.

While we continued to discuss "the issues," I vowed to go to Mass on the days we would see each other. In this way, I could receive Jesus into my body and then imitate Mary by bearing Christ to my friend through Jesus' Eucharistic Presence within me.

I could be a Christ-bearer. I could bring Christ to my friend in a way that transcended our differences and disagreements, and hopefully would penetrate his heart rather than just his intellect. That, I discovered, was the easy part.

One summer day, I had the privilege of praying with Babsie Bleasdell. Babsie is a dynamic preacher of the Word from Trinidad, West Indies, who has a grandmotherly and maternal heart. She was visiting Steubenville to speak at a conference, so I seized the opportunity to get together and pray about my relationship with my Eastern mystic.

After we prayed, I was driving to meet him and I heard in my spirit, "Pray to convert your romantic love into a maternal love." Needless to say, my first response was, "No way!"

Over the years, however, I've learned that whenever I'm resisting the Spirit, I should pray for the grace to be *willing* to pray for whatever is being asked of me. So I started praying: "Holy Spirit, help me be *willing* to pray to convert my romantic love into a maternal love."

Within two days my heart was changed, and I was praying sincerely to convert my romantic love into a maternal love. But then I had to ask, "What is a maternal love?"

Loving My Son

The answer came to me unexpectedly a couple weeks later as I was parking my car at work. I was sitting behind the steering wheel when suddenly I realized a maternal love is the way I love my son Michael: it is constant, unconditional, and doesn't expect my emotional needs to be met in return. My love for him is not up and down; it is not dependent on whether he is good or bad; nor do I expect him to care for my emotional needs.

Spiritual Motherhood Defined

I didn't realize it then, but the Holy Spirit was tutoring me in spiritual motherhood. In fact, it wasn't until I read John Paul II's "Letter to Women"[4] and "On the Dignity and Vocation of Women" that I discovered what I was doing had a name—that it was called **spiritual motherhood, and it meant nurturing the emotional, moral, cultural, and spiritual life of others.**

The Sky's the Limit

Once I understood this, I began to realize there were a zillion ways to express spiritual motherhood: smiling at someone in the grocery store, praying with my son on the way to the bus stop, teaching dance to senior citizens, making a meal for someone who's just had a baby, listening to a friend on the phone, and, my favorite way—giving roses to my women friends.

Another Hand of God

As I talked to other women and looked at their lives, I noticed they, too, were being spiritual mothers, often without realizing it. For instance, a friend named Patty, who is single, fiftyish, and a guidance counselor, is devoted to her students. She helps them know every educational, professional, and technical opportunity available to them. And since she is single, she considers whoever she is working with to be her family, to be the people God has given her to nurture and care for their well-being.

Patty puts it this way: "I'm not a mom, but that's okay because I have a lot of other titles—aunt, friend, godmother, guidance counselor, sister, and cousin. I try to be another hand of God on earth, to be there when people need me and to be generous with my time and love." Patty's grasped the heart of spiritual motherhood.

Seeing With the Heart

Then there's Maureen. Maureen married a faithful, loving Christian man and within a year was staying at home with their newborn son. Then the script started changing. At age two, her son was diagnosed with autism. That meant that day after day she had to deal with a hyperactive boy who flipped the lights on and off, who dumped toys in a huge pile in the middle of the floor and left them there, and who was still potty training at age five.

But Maureen learned to see Andrew with her heart. She learned to value his eternal destiny rather than getting frustrated over her son's earthly limitations. As a spiritual mother, she saw with the heart.

Maternal Glue

Finally, there's Mary Lou, who graduated from college in 1950, but didn't have the typical "Leave It to Beaver" marriage. Her husband owned a small grocery store where Mary Lou worked eight hours a day, five or six days a week. Yet even in the midst of her busyness, Mary Lou provided a glue, a cohesiveness, that knit her family of four children together.

Dinner time was sacred in her house—no running to soccer practice or out for a meeting. Every night Mary Lou cooked dinner, and every night the six of them gathered around the table to catch up on the day. This was the way Mary Lou nurtured the emotional, moral, and spiritual life of her children even in the midst of working.

Everyday Heroism

There are many, many other examples of spiritual motherhood, both among the saints and ordinary people. John Paul II called this type of living "everyday heroism." A significant part of this everyday heroism, he said, is the "silent but effective and eloquent witness of all those 'brave mothers who devote themselves to their own family without reserve, who suffer in giving birth to their children and who are ready to make any effort, to face any sacrifice, in order to pass on to them the best of themselves.'"[5]

This is a beautiful description of the self-giving of not only biological mothers, but of all women who give of themselves in the workplace, Church, neighborhood, and extended family. All women are called to give birth—physically and/or spiritually. All women are called to be Christ-bearers, to receive divine life in the womb of their souls and bear Christ to the world. All women are called to see in Mary's spiritual motherhood a reflection of their own lives.[6]

35

If every woman embraced the call to spiritual motherhood, it would be the nuclear reactor that would ignite the culture of life in the world. The feminine genius would be everywhere!

Every Woman's Call

It makes sense, then, that while some women are called to biological motherhood, **every woman is called to spiritual motherhood because motherhood is knit into the very structure of a woman's being.** Women are created with the gift of interior readiness to receive others into their lives, and in doing so, to nurture their emotional, moral, cultural, and spiritual well-being.

This is an exciting and creative challenge because women can be spiritual mothers anywhere—in the office, at home, with their grandchildren, in the neighborhood, even sick in bed.

A spiritual mother can be single, married, or widowed. She can have 10 children or no children, work in the home or out of the home. In fact, I find many women have already discovered this part of the journey. They're already being spiritual mothers without realizing it. They just didn't have a name for what they were doing.

No Doormats!

But I'd like to give a word of caution. When I first started speaking about spiritual motherhood, women thought I was telling them to be doormats, to let everyone walk all over them and to have no boundaries.

That's *not* what I'm saying. **Spiritual motherhood is not an indiscriminate gift of self** as if a woman has to give and give and give to whoever asks of her. A spiritual mother helps others grow into wholeness, not dependency. She nurtures the emotional, moral, cultural, and spiritual life of others so they can make a fuller gift of self to God and others, not so they can be irresponsible and self-indulgent. Sometimes the best thing a spiritual mother can do is say "no."

Open Wide the World to Women

Liberating the feminine genius is the passionate cry of John Paul II's messages to women. He was convinced that biological and spiritual motherhood could rebuild a civilization of love and a culture of life. That is why he said:

> "It is necessary to strive convincingly to ensure that the widest possible space is open to women in all areas of culture, economics, politics, and ecclesial life itself, so that all human society is increasingly enriched by the gifts proper to masculinity and femininity."[7]

Like leaven in the dough, the genius of women must bring its uplifting presence into the boardroom, courtroom, and classroom. Unceasingly, John Paul II pleaded for political and social change in order for women to fully share their gifts with the whole community and to be artisans of peace.[8]

Open Wide the Church to Women

Increasing women's participation in public and political life is only one-third of John Paul II's message to women. He also appealed to the whole Church community to "foster feminine participation in every way in its internal life."[9]

Just so we could understand the extent to which he expected the Church to foster this feminine participation, John Paul II enumerated the possibilities:

> "I am thinking, for example, of theological teaching, the forms of liturgical ministry permitted, including service at the altar, pastoral and administrative councils, Diocesan Synods and Particular Councils, various

ecclesial institutions, curias, and ecclesiastical tribunals, many pastoral activities, including the new forms of participation in the care of parishes when there is a shortage of clergy, except for those tasks that belong properly to the priest."[10] (More about women and the priesthood in chapter 8.)

Open Wide the Home to Women

But we must not misinterpret John Paul II. Promoting the presence and participation of women in all aspects of society and the Church should never be at the expense of the family. The importance of the family comprises the final third of his message.

The challenge facing most societies, he said, "is that of upholding, indeed strengthening, woman's role in the family while at the same time making it possible for her to use all her talents and exercise all her rights in building up society."[11]

A mother's presence in the family must be recognized, applauded, and supported, he reminded the world, while the misconception that motherhood "is oppressive to women, and...prevents a woman from reaching personal fulfillment, and...from having an influence on society" must be dispelled.[12]

Changing Culture

John Paul II was a both/and guy. He implored women to live out the feminine genius in the home *and* in public life *and* in the Church. Why all three? Because ultimately it is culture—the context in which we live life—that must change. And that context includes the home, the Church, and society.[13]

This is why John Paul II constantly called us to rebuild a culture of life and a civilization of love. He urged the whole Body of Christ to develop a culture that affirms women's dignity, and respects and welcomes femininity. Gender is not something to be eliminated. It is to be celebrated and accentuated.

Over 10 years ago, John Paul II invited women to "reflect carefully on what it means to speak of the *'genius of women,'* not only in order to be able to see in this phrase a specific part of God's plan which needs to be accepted and appreciated, but also in order to let this genius be more fully expressed in the life of society as a whole, as well as in the life of the Church."[14] That invitation is even more urgent today. Every woman is given the task of reflecting on her own feminine genius so as to unlock its spiritual dynamism for the Church, the family, and the world.

Defining the Feminine Genius

Although John Paul II never formally defined the feminine genius, I would describe it this way: **The feminine genius is the distinctive way a woman makes a gift of self in all her feminine fullness and originality as God intended her to be from the beginning.**

As women, we must not be swallowed up by a culture that tells us there's no real difference between men and women, nor can we succumb to a society that demeans women for their feminine distinctiveness. Rather, let us always keep in mind that every woman's journey is to live her feminine genius in an original and unique way, so as to bring into being that which never existed before—human life, spiritual life, and the fullness of emotional and cultural life.

ഇൗ

Questions for Reflection and Discussion

1. Before reading this chapter, what was your impression of John Paul II's view of women? Did your view change?

2. What do you think is the unique way a woman makes a sincere gift of self?

3. Have you ever thought of yourself as a spiritual mother? Why or why not?

4. How can you make spiritual motherhood a part of your everyday life?

5. How would you define the feminine genius?

Chapter 4

સ્Ж

Sin and the Nuptial Meaning of the Body

A couple years ago, I gave a talk on the nuptial meaning of the body at a parish in Pennsylvania. Afterwards, editor and writer Mike Aquilina sent me a cartoon portraying a surprised priest being confronted by an unfriendly customs official. The caption read: "That's right, Father. I said strip—right down to the nuptial meaning of your body."

No More Paradise

This was obviously a well-informed (but fictional) customs official. For most of us, the nuptial meaning of the body isn't a household word. When was the last time someone asked you, "So, how's the nuptial meaning of your body today?" We don't talk this way. Something happened on the journey between the "beginning" and today, and that something was original sin.

In his writings, John Paul II not only delved into the "genesis" of the human person (our creation in the image and likeness of God) and the "genius" of women (the way women make a distinctly feminine gift of self), he also addressed the "gouging" we've received as a result of original sin.

GO NY!!! Ruptured

To reflect on this gouging, John Paul II turned to Genesis 3 and the story of original sin. In this story, Satan tempts Eve not only with a sin of the intellect and emotions (to be like God), but with a sin of the body. He tempts her to eat the fruit and so involve her body in the first sin of mankind.

This is not a minor detail. Original sin indeed darkens the intellect and disorders the emotions, but it also ruptures our ability for union and communion through the body on four levels. These four levels of union are what the *Catechism of the Catholic Church* calls the four "harmonies"[1] and what I like to call "GO NY!!"

G = God

Sin ruptures our union and communion with *God*. When God shows up, Adam and Eve hide; they're afraid. John Paul II described the change in relationship this way: "Man turns his back on God-Love, on the Father. In a way, he casts God out of his heart."[2] At the end of Genesis 3, we see the ultimate rupture in our relationship with God: Adam and Eve are cast out of the garden, out of God's presence (Gen. 3:23).

O = Others

Sin ruptures our union and communion with *others*. When God asks Adam if he's eaten from the tree, he commits the original blame shift: "The woman whom you put here with me— she gave me fruit from the tree" (Gen. 3:12). Eve, in turns, blames the serpent. And the pattern goes on....

The rupture between man and woman is also highlighted in the consequences pronounced by God. He tells Eve, "Your desire will be for your husband and he will lord it over you" (Gen. 3:16b).[3] This foretells how some women will sacrifice their dignity for the sake of male attention and security, and how some men will use this desire to their advantage.

John Paul II likewise recognized this rupture: "After breaking the original covenant with God, the man and the woman found themselves more divided. Instead of being united, they were more opposed because of their masculinity and femininity."[4]

N = Nature

Sin ruptures our union and communion with *nature*. Every woman who labors to give birth ("in pain shall you bring forth children," Gen. 3:16a) and every man (and woman) who labors to earn a living ("by the sweat of your face shall you get bread to eat," Gen. 3:19) experiences this rupture.

Whereas God designed us to be fruitful in harmony with nature ("Be fertile and multiply; fill the earth and subdue it." Gen. 1:28), original sin introduced tension and conflict into our relationship with the created order. Fruitfulness won't happen without suffering. Here's how John Paul II described this conflict: "The words of God-Yahweh forewarn the hostility of the world, the resistance of nature with regard to man and his tasks."[5]

Y = Yourself

Sin ruptures the union and communion between body and spirit. This is evidenced by the birth of shame. Adam and Eve cover their bodies not because they have a sudden hankering for designer fig leaves, but because they feel exposed. Instead of experiencing the body as a sign of their self-giving union, the body is seen as an object to be used.

The body is clothed not because the body is bad, but because the body no longer radiates the spirit. Acknowledging the body/spirit split, John Paul II wrote: "A certain constituitive break within the human person is revealed, which is almost a rupture of man's original spiritual and somatic [bodily] unity. He realizes for the first time that his body has ceased drawing upon the power of the spirit."[6]

No Private Affair

Once again, Scripture is showing (rather than telling) a

profound truth: our ability for union and communion through a sincere gift of self has been ruptured. While Genesis 1 and 2 guided us on a visual journey of life "in the beginning," Genesis 3 provides a visual journey of life ruptured by sin. Through this journey we see that sin is never an individual affair. It profoundly affects the way we relate to God, to others, to the world around us, and even to our own bodies.

After sin, the body no longer leaps at the opportunity to make a sincere gift of self for union and communion, but leans toward the temptation to live apart from God's design. The traditional term "concupiscence" means exactly this—our "leaning" or "inclination" toward sin. As John Paul II observed, we are pulled "to satisfy the body, often at the cost of a real and full communion of persons."[7]

The Body Target

In the journey of life, we too are subject to this pull. Satan remains an ever-present foe, targeting our feminine bodies just as he targeted Eve's. As a result, Satan is after us again and again to sin in the body. If he can rupture our ability for union and communion through the body, then he's on his way to destroying the image of God in us.

Satan's Five Strategies

When it comes to women, Satan has at least five favorite strategies to tempt women to sin in the body. I like to call these the inferiority syndrome, the counterfeit-union syndrome, the 7–10 split syndrome, the freedom-from syndrome, and the appendix syndrome.

1) The Inferiority Syndrome

First, *the inferiority syndrome.* Many women have been bluntly told in school, the workplace, or even their own family that they were unwanted because they weren't born a boy or that they're inferior because they're not male. This message gets embedded into their self-concept, and the body, for these women, is not a source of joy and delight, but of pain and shame. This is also true for women who have been abused physically and/or emotionally by their fathers or men they trusted, or who have been neglected or abused by their mothers.

Burying the Body

Due to pain and shame, many women take their femininity and bury it deep in the ground like a coffin, hoping it will never resurface. Some women masculinize their bodies by adopting male standards of success, dress, and even loose morals to prove their "equality" or worth. Other women purposefully gain excessive weight to make their bodies ugly and undesirable.

John Paul II warned against masculinizing our bodies when he reminded women: "In the name of liberation from male 'domination,' women must not appropriate to themselves male characteristics contrary to their own feminine 'originality'.... If they take this path, women will not 'reach fulfillment,' but instead will *deform and lose their essential richness.*"[8]

In order to unmask Satan's masculinizing strategy, it's helpful to consider where we may have buried our feminine side because of pain and shame, or copied masculine ways of thinking and acting in order to compete or prove our worth. In doing so, we may have neglected the particular way we image God's presence in the world, which is our sensitivity to what is personal and relational.

2) The Counterfeit-Union Syndrome

But being relational isn't always easy, which brings us to the second way Satan tempts women through their bodies— *the counterfeit-union syndrome.* Because women are structured in their being for union, we yearn for intimacy with another, sometimes at the sacrifice of our own dignity and identity. As a result, we're tempted to use our bodies for counterfeit union.

The insidious thing about a counterfeit is that it looks like the real thing, smells like the real thing, and can even be used like the real thing. But it's not the real thing. It's a counterfeit.

When the FBI trains its agents to spot counterfeits, they study the real thing intensively. By exposing agents to what is authentic and genuine, counterfeits are easily identified. The imitation pales in comparison to the real thing.

Settling for Second Best

Unfortunately, many women are willing to settle for imitation intimacy. We use our bodies for counterfeit union through sexual relationships outside of marriage, cohabitation, homosexuality, and contraceptive use. It really shouldn't surprise us that homosexuality is on the rise. It's one of Satan's most effective weapons against the divine design. God designed us to image the Trinity by being one nature embodied in two ways, for the purpose of union and communion through a sincere and fruitful gift of self. Difference allows for fruitfulness.

With homosexuality, sameness (male/male or female/female) is preferred over difference. This "union" can never burst forth in the fruitfulness of a child, but remains sterile. Homosexuality and all false intimacy have this sterilizing effect. They encourage the counterfeit union of two individuals rather than the real communion of two persons.

Fashioned for Union

Often I ask myself, "Why are women so tempted by counterfeit union? Why do we remain in abusive and compromising situations?"

Our culture tells us it's because we love too much or because we're from Venus. Hogwash! It's because women are structured in their being for union and communion. The union of egg and sperm takes place within a woman's body. The unborn child is united to its mother through the umbilical cord. The newborn infant receives its nourishment by being connected to its mother's breast.

However, because original sin wounds the nuptial meaning of the body, women often don't know how to express their desire for union and intimacy other than through a romantic or sexual way.

Intimacy or Romance?

One of the biggest mistakes women make is *confusing intimacy with romance.* We think they're the same thing, and they're not. I might have gone my whole adult life confusing the two if it wasn't for Argentine tango.

One night, I danced a wonderful tango with a man. As the song ended, I remained in his arms with a warm, melted chocolate feeling. My thoughts drifted toward the ozone layer and thoughts of romance when I said to myself, "Time out, Katrina, you know this man! Off the dance floor he's arrogant, self-centered, and never asks you how you are. How could you even consider being romantic with him?"

That night taught me one of the most important lessons of my adult feminine life—the difference between intimacy and romance. Intimacy (for women) is the feeling of emotional closeness, of being safe, secure, and accepted in another's space. But romance is different. Romance moves toward an exclusive and permanent relationship with another that involves the total gift of self.

As women, we need to learn how to experience emotional closeness as a dimension of being made for union and communion while realizing it doesn't give us the green light to race into romance.

Women are created for emotionally intimate friendships. Otherwise we shrivel up and die. We become parched like a desert, and then a trickle of male attention comes our way and we soak it up. And before we know it, we're knee deep or waist deep or over our heads in counterfeit union.

Emotional Counterfeit Union

For married women, counterfeit union can take on an emotional dimension as well. If a married woman shares her intimate thoughts and feelings with a man who is not her husband, she can bond with him in a way that replaces or competes with her emotional marital bond. What began as an "innocent friendship" diverts more and more of a woman's emotional attention from her spouse to this emotionally nourishing relationship.

And since the physical dimension isn't involved, it can be harder to recognize the "friendship" as a trangression against the marital bond. And yet, it is. Despite the wrenching pain it will cause, women in these situations must sever the competing relationship.

What, then, is a woman in an emotionally barren marriage to do? Does she cut off all contact with men? Does she grit her teeth and embrace a life of emotional martyrdom?

Greater RDA

No, but she does have to turn to her feminine friendships to provide a sense of being cherished, of being connected and bonded with another.[9] Women have a much greater RDA than men, a much greater Relational Daily Allowance.

I know it sounds trite, but one man can never supply all of a woman's relational needs. Heck, one friendship can never supply all of a woman's relational needs. We need friends to go shopping with, friends to pray with, friends to hike with, and friends to cry with.

If we truly want to avoid counterfeit union, whether as married or single women, then developing feminine friendships must take center stage. As we do so, it will be easier and easier to make the distinction between intimacy and romance, and so avoid the hurtful trap of Genesis 3:16. ("Your desire will be for your husband [i.e., a man] and he will lord it over you.") And we can help our friends avoid this trap as well.

Starving for Union

Some women may never be tempted by counterfeit sexual or emotional union. Instead their desire for union finds a different avenue for expression: addiction.

A woman's craving for union and intimacy is so strong that when it goes unmet, it can pop up through addiction or other unhealthy attachments. Alcoholism, eating disorders, depression, self-stimulation, even workaholism and body building can be feminine attempts to numb or fill this unmet need for intimacy.

But, please, don't get obsessive about this. Just because a woman craves chocolate or buys a new couch doesn't necessarily mean she's starved for union. But I think it's worth looking at why women eat when they're upset, go shopping when there's a gnawing emptiness inside, or find themselves overcommitted. A woman's inability to say "no," whether it's to food, a garage-sale bargain, alcohol, or volunteering, often has its roots in her intense, but usually subconscious, desire for union and communion.

3) The 7-10 Split Syndrome

Unfortunately, modern culture doesn't help women understand and integrate this desire for union and intimacy very well. Instead, it helps Satan bombard women with his third attack: *the 7-10 split syndrome.*

If you've ever gone bowling, you've probably experienced the 7-10 split. This happens when you roll the ball, hit the head pin smack in the center, and end up with the 7 pin on one side and the 10 pin on the other side.

This is what Satan wants to do with us. He's constantly hitting us on the "head pin"—hitting our minds and emotions to get the body on one side and the spirit on the other. He wants us to forget the body has any spiritual meaning, and to think the body is just...a body.

Woman or Object?

How does he do this? Turn on the TV. Look at billboards. Read *Cosmopolitan.* Pick up a romance novel. Watch MTV. (Okay, *don't* watch MTV.) Television, music, advertisements, and movies completely ignore the spiritual dimension of a woman. Rather than portraying women as spiritually alive and open to new life within the covenant of marriage, pop culture zeros in on the physical dimension. Women are reduced to an object to be used for sexual gratification and pleasure apart from God's design.

John Paul II was keenly aware of this reductionistic approach: "It is one thing to be conscious that the value of sex [i.e., sexual relations] is part of all the rich storehouse of values with which the female appears to the man. It is another to 'reduce' all the personal riches of femininity to that single value, that is, of sex, as a suitable object for the gratification of sexual activity itself."[10]

Only Matter

Even the "scientific experts" contribute to the 7-10 split. They assume the body is mere biology, just a highly evolved collection of molecules and organs that keeps you breathing, walking, talking, etc.

And since there's no deeper spiritual significance to the body, you have every right to do with it whatever you want. In fact, it would be *irresponsible* not to use birth control or sterilization to control your fertility. After all, if science and technology have figured out a way to do it, then why not?

If your body was just biology, this would be true. Do whatever you want with your body; do whatever you want with someone else's body. Use science and technology to cut up, tie off, and take out healthy parts of the body. It's only matter.

More Than Biology

But we're not just biology. We're not just matter. We're human persons who image God through body and spirit. It really matters what you do with your matter! Despite what the media, science, and well-meaning people in the Church have said, contraception, sterilization, abortion, and test tube babies are not blessings of modern technology. They are part of Satan's plan to split your body from your spirit, to reduce you and your body to merely the physical dimension.

A Sacred Sign

In God's design, **a woman's body and her fertility are not just biology; they also have a spiritual reality.** The feminine body is designed by God to be a sacred sign, to reveal God. A woman's body, mind, spirit, and fertility united together image the Trinity—the fruitful, self-giving love of the Trinity.

A Sterile God

Contraception, abortion, and sterilization depict a different image of God to the world—a sterile image. The love between the Father and Son no longer bursts forth in the fruitfulness of another Person, but is self-contained. God is not a fruitful Trinity, but a sterile duality. The Holy Spirit is contracepted out of the Trinity. The procreative genius of woman is put on the back burner or eliminated altogether. The sexual act is reduced to only its physical dimension.

The 7-10 split syndrome makes a contraceptive, anti-woman culture possible. It barrages us with a view of reality where it's perfectly acceptable to split the body from the spirit, to make the other into an object for our pleasure. Sadly, this split allows women to be used in the marital covenant and outside of it, to have all the personal riches of her femininity reduced to a single value.

To Be Loved or to Be Used?

This is a difficult message to hear and absorb. It calls for a change, and few of us like to be asked to change. God, however, never demands. He invites. He appeals to our hearts and minds, and most of all to our dignity and free will. **God wants all women to be loved rather than used.** He wants our journey to be one of reuniting body and spirit into a life-giving whole rather than dividing ourselves into disconnected, sterile pieces. He desires the sacred reality of the feminine body and its ability to image God to be the source of true happiness and freedom.

4) The Freedom-From Syndrome

Redefining happiness and freedom is precisely the goal of Satan's fourth strategy—*the "freedom-from" syndrome.*

Have you ever noticed that freedom in the media is usually portrayed as a "freedom from"? Freedom from responsibility and housework; freedom from Church rules; freedom from fat, wrinkles, and old age spots. This type of unrestricted freedom, the media promises, will make you happy.

In the Service of Love

It's funny how we never hear about the freedom *to*—the freedom to love unconditionally, to suffer without bitterness, to not compare ourselves, to make a sincere gift of self. This type of freedom refuses to make itself into an absolute. It always places freedom in the service of love. The goal of Christian freedom is not more freedom, but love. It's love that makes us happy, not unrestricted freedom.

Perhaps you might like to take a moment and ask yourself, "What does freedom mean to me?" Am I tempted to think of freedom as getting rid of restrictive rules and regulations? Do I dream of happiness apart from pregnancy or housework? Do I think getting a better paying job or a bigger house will bring me real freedom? Am I waiting for the day I lose 30 pounds or Prince Charming rescues me from the single life?

These struggles are real, and yet the answer is not fully found in "freedom from." It's found in the freedom *to* encounter God and make a sincere gift of self even before you lose 30 pounds or even as you trudge to work day after day. It's the freedom to live passionately even before Prince Charming arrives or to welcome an unexpected child. It's the freedom to love in the midst of imperfect and unanticipated situations.

5) *The Appendix Syndrome*

And finally, Satan's fifth strategy: *the appendix syndrome.* In reaction to society's obsession with sex and physical appearance, many Christian women go to the opposite extreme and overspiritualize. We downplay our bodies.

How many of us have been tempted to think, "Oh, if only I could get rid of my body I'd be more holy!" We can't wait to shed the body like a snake skin and leave it behind at death. We think the soul is what truly images God and the body is rather unnecessary, kind of like an appendix. We're tempted to think our identity wouldn't really change if the body was removed. In fact, we'd be better off without it!

Saving Souls

Unfortunately, this thinking has crept into our spiritual language. For instance, I often hear the expression, "Jesus came to save souls." I hate to say this, he didn't. Jesus came to save *persons*. As Christians we believe our salvation will not be complete until soul and body are united with the Lord forever in heaven. Jesus came to save you as a person, not just a soul without a body. So get used to your body; it'll be with you for all eternity!

Heavenly Bodies

Recently I spoke with a friend about her parish's reaction to this last comment. Many of the women were puzzled. They didn't understand what I meant about our bodies going to heaven with us. They thought the body returned to ash and remained ash. It was just temporary housing. End of discussion.

I'm reminded again how many Christians misunderstand the body. If the body is just temporary housing, it doesn't matter if we ignore it, starve it, sterilize it, or excessively pierce it. In fact, it doesn't even matter if it's male or female. After all, some day we'll be rid of it and then we'll finally be free.

Not Generic

Jesus didn't get rid of his body. It was glorified. And in that glorified state, it was still *his* body. His wounds remained. He said to Thomas, "Take your finger and examine my hands. Put your hand into my side. Do not persist in your unbelief, but believe!" (Jn. 20:27). Our glorified body will be *our* body, not someone else's body or a generic body. **Somehow our resurrected body will resemble the body we have on earth.**

What does the glorified body look like? No one knows for sure, but when responding to this question, Paul wrote to the Corinthians: "The splendor of the heavenly bodies is one thing, that of the earthly another.... What is sown in the earth is subject to decay, what rises is incorruptible.... A natural body is put down and a spiritual body comes up" (1 Cor. 15:40, 42, 44).

The glorified and natural body are the same and different. As John Paul II said many times, the body expresses the person, it expresses the spirit.[11] We image God by being both body and spirit. This is true on earth *and* in heaven, even though in heaven, body and spirit are transformed in a completely new way.

The Body Reveals God

The process, however, of transforming our bodies into a spiritual one begins even now. We've all seen or met someone who radiates the Spirit. People flocked to Blessed Teresa of Calcutta ("Mother Teresa") because God emanated from her body. John Paul II lived only to glorify God in his body even while his body was ravaged by Parkinson's disease and compromised by slurred speech.

The work of salvation on earth is not getting rid of our bodies, but allowing God to be revealed ("glorified") through our bodies. Jesus, the Second Person of the Blessed Trinity, revealed God by taking on flesh. John 1:14 says it so clearly: "The Word became flesh and made his dwelling among us, and we have seen his glory: The glory of an only Son coming from the Father." In John 14:9, Jesus tells his disciples: "Whoever has seen me [i.e., my body] has seen the Father."

The same is true of us. We "take on flesh" so that we can reveal God. In St. Paul's words: "You must know that your body is a temple of the Holy Spirit who is within.... So glorify [reveal] God in your body" (1 Cor. 6:19-20).

How to Image Body and Soul

Cathedral of the Soul

If, then, we're suppose to befriend our bodies even on this

earthly journey, how is that possible? Here's the way I love to image the relationship between body and soul: **the soul is the tabernacle of the body and the body is the cathedral of the soul.**

We would never place a tabernacle out in the open, exposed to everything around it. Likewise, it would be impossible to have a cathedral without a tabernacle because it's no longer a sacred space. The tabernacle needs the cathedral, and the cathedral needs the tabernacle. The two go together. So, too, the soul needs the body, and the body needs the soul. They go together.

Eucharist of the Body

A second image I love is that of the monstrance and the Eucharist. The monstrance is a beautiful holder used for Eucharistic Adoration, often in the shape of a sunburst. The Eucharist is placed at its center. Using this image we could say **the body is the monstrance of the soul and the soul is the Eucharist of the body.**

The purpose of the monstrance is to display and enhance the beauty of the Eucharist. Likewise, the purpose of the body is to display and enhance the beauty of the soul. They don't compete with each other. They *complete* each other to bring out their shared beauty and brilliance.

Redemption of the Body

In order to heal the effects of sin and resist Satan's strategies, we have to start here—with the cathedral of our bodies. Many women struggle with their identity as a daughter and as a woman precisely because they struggle with their bodies.

We need the grace to love and reverence our bodies, not just tolerate them. We need to understand it is through the body that we image God. And most importantly, we have to be healed of shame, self-hatred, addiction, and hurtful memories that prevent us from living in union and communion with God, others, nature, and within ourselves between body and spirit.

Our God is not only a saving God, but a healing God. He's deeply aware of our feminine wounds and our intense need to be loved and accepted. He wants to bring us close to his wounded side, to cleanse our memories, and to heal the gaping wounds that ravage our hearts.

St. Paul says, "If anyone is in Christ, he is a new creation. The old order has passed away; now all is new!" (2 Cor. 5:17). Every woman's journey must pass through the loving gaze of the Father as well as the grace of the cross. Our entire being is meant to be born again from the wounded side of Christ. The Christian journey is not only the redemption of the spirit, but the redemption of the body as well.

Healing Body and Soul

To end this chapter, I invite you to find a quiet place and pray the following meditation:

> Lord, I come to you this day and ask you to renew my life. Take me into the womb of your heart so that I may be reborn from the side of Christ. As you rebirth me into the world, may the water and blood that flowed from your side wash and purify my memory, emotions, understanding, and will. May it strip away the anger, hurt, and resentment encasing my heart toward those who have ridiculed, rejected, or abused me because of my femininity.

> Please remove every feeling of self-despising, condemnation, and self-rejection embedded within me and replace them with a peace and acceptance of who you made me to be from the beginning.

Lord, I repent for trying to satisfy my desires for union and intimacy through counterfeit union or sexual relations outside of marriage. You know how much I long to be one with another! I give these longings to you and ask you to satisfy them. I am sorry for the times I've allowed my body to be used as an object, for failing to stand up for my own dignity, and for betraying my unique ability to give life.

Please send your Holy Spirit to liberate me from Satan's strategies that would blind me and distract me from my true dignity and vocation as a woman in the world.

Lord, I want to reveal you through my body. Help me to come forth from your side with all the beauty and purity of a bride adorned for her wedding, so that I can be the temple of the Holy Spirit that you created me to be. Thank you, Jesus, for loving me and coming to re-create me right now, at this moment, in this place.

ᏕᎧᏖᎸ

Questions for Reflection and Discussion

1. How have you experienced sin disrupting your ability to make a sincere gift of self to God and others?

2. Have you ever struggled with any of the five syndromes: inferiority, counterfeit-union, 7-10 split, freedom-from, or appendix? Are there other ways you've struggled with your body?

3. Does the image of cathedral and tabernacle or monstrance and Eucharist help you understand better the relationship between body and soul? Can you think of another image to describe this relationship?

4. Are there areas in your life that need to be reborn from the side of Christ?

Chapter 5

ഇറാങ്

Weaving a Tapestry of Life

*L*iving the fullness of womanhood is tough. We have to recover our identity as daughters of the Father, be awakened to the feminine genius, and healed of the wounds that paralyze and misshape our feminine identity. We might be tempted to think the journey is over. And yet, the river rushes on.

Living in Process

A number of years ago when my son misbehaved, I ripped into him like a chainsaw into a tree. He fled crying to his room while I sat in the kitchen tormented by guilt, remorse, and failure. Unexpectedly, the Holy Spirit slipped a thought into my heart: "The process is just as important as the end product."

In that moment, I realized I could stampede my son into acting the way I wanted, but to what avail? The *process* of disciplining him was the real arena where values and virtues were passed on.

This insight changed my interactions with my son *and* my life. I began repeating to myself: "The process is just as important as the end product." Soon, even that paradigm had to shift when God showed me: **"The process *is* the end product."**

I had to stop racing toward the future or pining for the past. I had to live in the present moment and love the journey.

Are We There Yet?

I find it difficult to love the journey. I'd much rather arrive than be on my way. However, that pesky fly from chapter 1 won't let me "arrive." I keep finding myself asking, "Who am I?" because who I am at 18 is different from 25 or 35 or 65 or 85. The journey continues. The Holy Spirit beckons on. So, what's next?

Having been married for 10 years, it was agonizing to have my marriage fail and redefine myself as a single person. It felt so awkward. I didn't fit in with single people because I had a family. I didn't fit in with married people because I didn't have a husband.

Not only that, shortly after my marriage failed, the Catholic community around which everything in my life had been woven as a seamless garment was also wrenched in two.

Fragments Everywhere

Suddenly, everything wasn't neatly connected. In fact, my life was in fragments—the fragments of work, parish life, and what was left of community life; the fragments of cooking, housecleaning, mowing the lawn, and paying bills; the fragments of my son's school, redefined relationships, and single parenting. Rather than a nice, tidy seamless garment, I had a rather disconnected patchwork quilt.

It was very humbling. With the shoe of divorce on my foot, with our exalted Catholic community brought low, my pride took a deadly blow. I used to think, "Look at my life—with a little more effort and self-discipline, you can do it too." Now I was simply hanging on for dear life, trying not to come apart at the seams because I was pulled in so many different directions.

The patchwork-quilt stage went on for about four years as I collected pieces and tried to find ways to bind them together.

During this time, a very important piece of the quilt came to me from Dr. Ronda Chervin, a Catholic woman philosopher in the United States. She introduced me to another Catholic woman philosopher, St. Edith Stein, a Carmelite nun who died in a Nazi concentration camp and was canonized in 1998 by Pope John Paul II.

U-G-I

In her essays on women, St. Edith Stein described three levels of vocation.[1] First, every person has a universal vocation (U), a vocation we share in common with all people. Secondly, we each have a vocation according to gender (G), whether we are male or female. And thirdly, we have an individual vocation (I), one that is uniquely ours.

When I learned about these three vocations, the pieces of my fractured life started to make more sense. It was like turning a kaleidoscope and having the pieces fall into place to make a pattern. And, in fact, it's these three vocations that provide the framework for this book.

Daughter of the Father

Our first vocation, the universal vocation we share in common with everyone, is that we are children of God. This is what God showed me on my thirtieth birthday when he told me I was first a daughter, then a bride. Chapter 1 explored our universal vocation by reflecting on a woman's foundational identity as a daughter of the Father.

The Genius of Woman

Our second vocation is our vocation according to gender. Chapters 2 and 3 focused on this vocation. In these chapters we saw how women are created for union and communion through a feminine gift of self. We are created with an empty space within, to be receptive, to be life-bearers. Motherhood is knit into the very structure of our being. This means every woman, single or married, is called to maternity—emotional, moral, cultural, and spiritual maternity. This is a woman's second vocation.

Uniquely What?

But what about the third vocation, that vocation which is uniquely ours? Because my life was composed of competing patchwork squares as mother, writer, friend, cook, dancer, teacher, maintenance man, etc., I felt parceled out. None of these "roles" encompassed me fully.

When I began to look at my life as three levels of vocation instead of just one, I was greatly relieved. I didn't have to have one, grand, all-encompassing vocation in order for my life to make sense. I could operate out of the first two levels as a daughter of the Father and a woman while waiting for God to reveal the third level.

What about this third vocation? What's an intelligent, single mom like me to do? More of the answer came to me in a most unexpected way.

Snow Lessons

One October, I decided to buy a small '85 Honda Civic and put my mini-van up for sale. I paid for the Honda with my credit card, thus giving me two months to sell the mini-van and pay off my credit card. No problem.

That October weekend it started snowing, and it didn't stop for five months. When it snows in my part of Ohio, nobody car shops. We hibernate in our warm houses and do the minimum amount of driving. When Christmas rolled around, I still had two cars and a significant credit card debt. It was time for Plan B.

I contacted two of my sisters with very comfortable living standards and requested to borrow $1,000 and pay it back in six months. In response, they accused me of financial irresponsibility, poor planning, and living beyond my means.

I was shocked, hurt, and demeaned. However, their reactions launched me on an extensive self-examination: Was I being irresponsible? Unreasonable? Was I failing to plan for my financial future? Why didn't I have more money? What was important to me now and in the future?

Immeasurable Values

What I realized is that my sisters, both being scientists, value that which could be measured, that which could be seen. For me, the intangibles were more important—listening to a friend, walking my son to the bus stop, teaching confirmation, leaving a cheerful note for a coworker.

My life was poured out not on those things that could be measured and therefore prove I had used my time responsibly, but on enriching the lives of others and helping carry their burdens. To me, the intangibles were so much more important than the tangibles. My values and worth were not determined by what could be seen and measured and therefore "prove" I had used my time responsibly.

This added one more piece to the already complicated patchwork quilt I felt my life to be. Now that I understood the intangibles were important to me—things such as friendship, wholeness, spiritual growth, and emotional nourishment—what did I do with these? And how did I reconcile this with all the other demands on my life?

Opposites Go Together

I was bemoaning all this to a priest one day, and he introduced me to a concept St. Bonaventure called the coincidence of opposites. I like to call it the co-existence of opposites. It's very simple and it goes like this: Within ourselves we experience opposite desires and traits. We experience a desire for union and independence; to be among people and to be alone; to be generous and to be self-protective; to be patient and to act impulsively. We experience both transcendence and limitation.

According to Bonaventure, this is the way we're created, with this co-existence of opposites. I kept thinking something was wrong with me because I had all these "competing" desires: I am a Christian, and I love to dance tango. I love nature, and I love the city. I love philosophy, and I love flag football. I love to travel, and I have to mow the lawn. I'm a mom, and I'm a wage-earner.

I thought I had to choose one side over the other, one extreme over the other. With this new insight of the co-existence of opposites, I realized it wasn't an either/or situation but a both/and. I can love the transcendent and live in the concrete. I can value the intangibles and appreciate the tangibles.

Born Again Tapestry

I came away from that meeting with a whole new view of myself. I felt reconstituted, born again on the inside. I suddenly realized I no longer felt like a patchwork quilt. Now my life was a beautiful tapestry with each thread expressing a different part of who I am and woven together to make a beautiful picture.

I also realized something else. Whenever I thought of my life as a seamless garment, I'd always pictured it as a solid, burlap brown. When I thought of the patchwork quilt, it was various squares of color pasted together, but making no overall picture. Now, as a tapestry, there were beautiful oranges, vibrant reds, rich peacock blues. And **what made the tapestry beautiful were the contrasts between the different colors.**

Loving Contrast

For the first time, I began to welcome contrast in my life

and not feel as if I had to make everything the same. I can love the universal and the concrete. I can be fully alive as a Christian and pursue my love of dance. I can be a single mother and a wage earner. I can live in the city and love nature. The internal war was over and both sides had won. Hallelujah!

My Uniqueness

It may seem like I've gone far afield, but actually this relates back to my unique vocation. Through this process of selling the van (which, by the way, sold after six months to someone who wanted to buy it the first month, but couldn't), I learned how I am put together on the inside, how God has uniquely created Katrina Zeno: I live for the intangibles, for that which can't be measured in dollars and cents as in a well-furnished home or a high job position.

But I also learned that the concrete is very important. I have to learn to love the concrete because it is through the concrete—through a hug, a beautiful sunset, an exquisite dance, a homeless person—that we encounter the intangibles. As a friend of mine delights in saying, "I'm changing the world one diaper at a time."

Weaving a New Life

What does this mean for you who have journeyed with me from a seamless garment to a patchwork quilt to a colorful tapestry? I think it means there's a beautiful tapestry in you waiting to be discovered. God wants to take what might seem like a jumbled life of carpooling, housework, professional responsibilities, homeschooling, wage-earning, and elderly parent caretaking and weave it into something beautiful.

God wants to reawaken dimensions of your life you've either discarded because you're a wife and mother or disregarded because you're *not* a wife and mother. He wants to give your whole self back to you. He's inviting you to love the spiritual and the concrete.

More Than a Cog

Some of you reading this are probably nodding your heads and saying, "Yes, yes!" Others may be scratching your heads and wondering what the fuss is about. It's this: after our children are no longer young or we've toiled in the professional world for 15 or 20 years, we find ourselves asking again, "Who am I?"

That pesky fly returns to question whether our value and identity go deeper than the roles we play or the functions we perform. Otherwise we would be replaceable cogs in the grinding gears of the universe.

If being a replaceable cog disturbs you, I applaud you. You've sensed what John Paul II loved to say about each of us, that we are unique and unrepeatable.

You are unrepeatable. There's no one else like you in the world. No one else can fill your shoes. No one else was born at this time in history with your particular gifts, temperament, and life experience. You have a unique vocation. You are a unique tapestry. You are not a replaceable cog.

Unique But Hidden

The challenge, of course, is realizing this unique vocation doesn't mean we're going to be famous or celebrated. Most often it means we'll live hidden, uncelebrated lives. Who ever hears of the woman in Magadan, Siberia, struggling to feed her children or the woman professor in Slovakia teaching Christian psychology? Yet, each life is a unique strand in the divine tapestry, an indispensable part of the beauty of creation whose absence would leave a gaping hole.

One Person Makes a Difference

A story I heard recently reconvinced me of each person's value and the unique contribution we make to the divine tapestry. In pre-war Poland, there was a poor family who had two sons. The family only had enough money for the older son to be educated as a priest although the younger son also wanted to be a priest.

One day, the mother, who was a midwife, needed some medicine for a patient, but the local pharmacist had run out. The younger son ran all the way to the next town to ask that pharmacist for the necessary medicine.

When this pharmacist saw the young boy's willing spirit and spark for life, he inquired about his family and future desires. The boy confessed he wanted to be a priest, but the family couldn't afford the education. The pharmacist instructed the boy to go home and tell his parents that he (the pharmacist) would be willing to educate the boy in Latin and the other necessary subjects without charge.

This is precisely what happened, and the boy became St. Maximilian Kolbe, the Franciscan priest who inspired millions through his love of Mary and the giving of his life in exchange for another prisoner in the concentration camp of Auschwitz.

Lifetime Endeavor

This is how saints and tapestries are made: using the ordinary events of daily life. This is also how our unique vocation unfolds: through the ordinary (and sometimes not so ordinary) events of daily life. Our unique vocation isn't a do-it-yourself kit we discover one day, assemble, and it's done. Our unique vocation unfolds throughout our lifetime.

Events, hardships, broken hearts, hidden talents, joys, and gifts all conspire to keep our life flowing around the next bend. Sometimes the current is calm; other times it's turbulent. Some stretches are shallow, others deep. Sometimes the scenery bursts forth in awe-inspiring mountains; other times it reveals scruffy oaks and barren patches.

Through it all, one thing in life is predictable: change. Not only that, things change and change again. Change, however, isn't arbitrary. God allows the stretching, fracturing, and reconfiguring of our lives in order to weave our unique tapestries in a more holistic (and holy) way.

Heavenly Uniqueness

For me, the most astonishing fact about our unique vocation is that it continues even in heaven. Our personal uniqueness will not be absorbed in heaven, John Paul II assured us, but will stand out to an incomparably greater and fuller extent.[2]

Wow! That means who we are as unique and unrepeatable persons is accentuated in heaven, not diminished. This compels me to take my uniqueness seriously, to develop my human and artistic talents as absolutely necessary to the journey of my salvation and that of others.

Living the Process

As I've tried to live this process of embracing my unique vocation, three thoughts strike me:

1) Running on Empty

One of the greatest obstacles to our unique vocation unfolding is exhaustion and depletion. It's impossible for a woman's uniqueness to unfold if she feels nothing's there, if the needle is way past empty.

This experience of exhaustion and depletion is the most common complaint I hear among women with small children or who are working full time and raising a family. I think we'd be overspiritualizing if we ignored these feelings, so how do we remedy the situation?

From Channel to Reservoir

One way is to change the way we view ourselves. I used to think of myself as a channel through which grace flowed to others. I kept nothing for myself. I was simply a conduit. Then I heard that St. Bernard of Clairvaux says we should be reservoirs that pour out of our overflow.

If we're called to be reservoirs, we have to be replenished in order to continue giving out of our overflow. If nothing flows into the reservoir, it's only a matter of time until we're empty and barren.

Unfortunately, many of us walk around empty and depleted because of guilt. But it's not real guilt; it's false guilt. Real guilt convicts us that we acted wrongly, that we have sinned against God and others.

False guilt is a nagging voice that tells us we should be doing something else. It doesn't reveal objective wrongdoing, but accuses us of being unproductive and self-indulgent. It pops up when we choose stillness over activity, "no" over "yes," receiving over giving.

Coming Out of Hibernation

Here's the challenge: if we really believe God has a unique vocation for us, that we've been given a unique personality and gifts and have been born at this time in history for a reason, then we need to allow this uniqueness to unfold.

We need to slay false guilt and give ourselves permission to ask: How am I uniquely created? What are my personal interests and gifts? What replenishes me? Do I like to ski, garden, play the piano, play tennis, read a book? Am I interested in politics, counseling, natural medicine, or calligraphy? What were my dreams as a young girl? What talents or gifts have gone into hibernation?

More Than a Role

Even just asking these questions provokes twinges of guilt and sighs of impossibilities. The days are crammed with rushing kids off to school, rushing to work, rushing to get dinner ready.

The Holy Spirit must convince us that developing who we are as unique persons *apart from the roles we play* is honoring who God made us to be. It's reawakening our unique vocation from its mid-life slumber.

So be creative. Put your feminine genius to work. See if you can figure out common interests with your husband, children, roommates, or friends to find things that uniquely express who you are. Over the years, my son has danced with me, gone horseback riding, and played cards and games. I've attempted roller blade hockey (I don't recommend it), basketball, and playing catcher for his fast ball (ouch).

If you don't share common interests with your husband, children, or roommates, figure out ways they can make a sincere gift of self to you by freeing up an hour or two a week for the things that replenish you.

Richer and Fuller

I know this is hard for most women, and it even feels unnatural. Women find it excruciating to ask others to sacrifice for them. We'd rather inconvenience ourselves than inconvenience others.

However, please remember you are asking others to make a gift of self to you not so you can be self-indulgent, but so you can make a richer and fuller gift of your *unique* self back to God, your family, friends, and the world.

2) Productivity vs. Fruitfulness

As you begin embracing more of your unique vocation, you may find the Holy Spirit changes your thinking from being productive to being fruitful.

Checklist Value

Most of us are familiar with being productive. We constantly evaluate our days according to how many things we checked off our checklist or palm pilot. If we checked off a lot, we had a good day. If we checked off only two or three, it wasn't such a good day. I think God has a different vision by which he wants us to view ourselves, and that's the vision of fruitfulness.

This became apparent to me in May 1998 when I left my job as a publications writer for Franciscan University of Steubenville in Ohio. I felt it necessary to resign so I could pursue my unique vocation as a speaker and writer of Catholic spirituality. I grappled with this decision for almost two years due to my need to provide for my family and my past experience of appearing "irresponsible."

Fruitfulness of the Spirit

That same month, I read a book on the Blessed Mother by Fr. Marie-Dominique Philippe, OP, in which he described the Holy Spirit choosing Mary as his spouse to act in fruitfulness with her.[3] I couldn't keep reading. I had to put the book down and let this sentence convert me. The Holy Spirit was moving in my heart, telling me he wanted to do the same with me. He wanted to act in fruitfulness with me.

Not surprisingly, this same thought was echoed by John Paul II: "Only Mary and Joseph, who had lived the mystery of his [Jesus'] conception and birth, became the first witnesses of a fruitfulness different from that of the flesh, that is, of a fruitfulness of the Spirit."[4]

Linear vs. Spiral

This led me to reflect further on the difference between productivity and fruitfulness. Most of my life I've been very productive. This implies a linear idea of progress—a beginning, middle, and end that's accomplished in a straightforward sequence. At the end, something tangible and measurable is produced, which didn't necessarily require the cooperation of others to accomplish.

Fruitfulness is different. Fruitfulness is a hidden process, one that is spiral rather than linear. Sometimes it takes awhile for fruitfulness to take shape because nothing visibly emerges at first.

Fruitfulness also implies the cooperation of others. We're not fruitful by ourselves. A plant doesn't produce fruit by its own efforts but by a whole combination of factors. When a fruit matures, it isn't usually weighed and measured, but simply admired and appreciated.

A Different Standard

This is how I'm trying to look at my life now—that God is calling me to be fruitful. If at first my efforts aren't producing anything measurable, it's okay. In fact, it may take a while for the fruit to mature, but that doesn't mean I'm being irresponsible or nonproductive. It just means I'm being fruitful.

I'd like to give one word of warning: Living a fruitful life is tough! It's countercultural. It takes fortitude and perseverance because most people don't understand fruitfulness according to the Spirit.

Threefold Healing

However, fruitfulness according to the Spirit is incredibly healing. It spills over into each of St. Edith Stein's three vocations: Living our unique vocation heals the rupture between body and spirit. Living our vocation as women heals the rupture between us and others. And living our vocation as a daughter of the Father heals the rupture between us and God

I can see this happening in me now. As I embrace more fully my unique vocation, there's no longer a disconnect between who I am and what I do. More and more, they are the same thing. At times, I experience an incredible oneness of body and spirit that is so freeing, passionate, and full of life that I want to shout with St. Symeon the New Theologian: "I see how I was and what I have become. O wonder!"[5]

3) O Fiat!

Finally, to end this chapter, I'd like to turn to Mary and her unique life call. The German theologian Hans Urs von Balthasar wrote this about Mary: "Mary opens up countless possibilities of saying 'yes' for all who come after her. All of them are personal, all of them are original; according to God's commission, all of them are new and have never existed before.... For the Christian, above all else, is a man [woman] who says 'Yes.'"

By saying "yes" to God, Mary was faithful to her unique vocation. She opened up new possibilities for God's plan of salvation to be realized.

Your Fiat Counts

The same is true for each of us. God is writing an original script with each of our lives. He's not writing a remake or adaptation of someone else's life but something never before written. Through each of us, God wants to open up countless possibilities of saying "yes" for all who come after us. **Never underestimate the power and fruitfulness of your "yes" to God!**

Daughter, Woman, Unique Tapestry

If then, we combine everything we've reflected on so far, a woman is first a daughter of the Father. This is her universal vocation.

Secondly, she is created to make a feminine and sincere gift of self to others, especially through spiritual motherhood. This is her vocation according to gender.

Finally, every woman is entrusted with a unique vocation, a beautiful tapestry composed of a variety of colors and contrasts that is woven throughout the course of her life using her unique circumstances, struggles, gifts, and talents. Through her unique "yes," she opens up countless possibilities for fruitfulness through the Holy Spirit.

The Master Weaver

Our unique tapestry is a creative endeavor. It's also a mystery and tribute to God's sovereignty and self-giving love. On the one hand, we are filled with hope. On the other hand, pain and suffering stretch our faith beyond human limits, and we want to cry, "Lord, I believe. Help my unbelief!" (cf. Mk. 9:24).

I am indebted to the unknown author of the following poem, who beautifully captures everything I've been trying to say but in a surpassingly elegant manner. As you read it, may you sense the Master's hand weaving together the threads of your life.

"The Plan of the Master Weaver"

Our lives are but fine weavings
That God and we prepare,
Each life becomes a fabric planned
And fashioned in His care.
We may not always see just how
The weavings intertwine,
But we must trust the Master's hand
And follow his design.
For He can view the pattern
Upon the upper side,
While we must look from underneath

And trust in Him to guide...
Sometimes a strand of sorrow
Is added to His plan,
And though it's difficult for us,
We still must understand
That it's He who fills the shuttle,
It's He who knows what's best,
So we must weave in patience
And leave to Him the rest...
Not til the loom is silent
And the shuttle ceases to fly
Shall God unroll the canvas
And explain the reason why—
The dark threads are as needed
in the Weaver's skillful hand
As the threads of gold and silver
In the pattern He has planned.

ഋഐ

Questions for Reflection and Discussion

1. Which image do you identify with the most at this time in your life: seamless garment, patchwork quilt, or tapestry?

2. Is there another image you would use to describe your life at this moment? (mosaic, garden, battered car, empty glass, chalice, etc.) Why?

3. How does the concept of three vocations change the way you look at your life?

4. Do you have a sense of what your unique vocation might be?

5. What prevents your uniqueness from unfolding?

6. Are you able to replenish the reservoir periodically, or is it more often depleted?

7. Do you evaluate yourself more according to productivity or fruitfulness? Would you like to change this standard of evaluation? How?

8. How would you answer the question "Who am I?" at this point in your life?

Chapter 6

ഓരൂ

The Spouse of the Spirit

*W*oven into every woman's unique tapestry is an incredibly strong yearning for intimacy and union. This thread accounts for the peaks and valleys of most women's lives.

When a woman feels close to someone, she feels alive, energized, and valued. When she feels alienated and isolated from others, life can be a living hell. Simple tasks are draining. Her emotional pulse is flat. She wonders if the journey is even worth living.

Obviously we don't experience mountain-top intimacy every moment of our lives. But does this mean we aren't living in union with God and others? Is it possible to live moment-by-moment union even when we don't live perpetually on the mountain-top?

Beyond Daughter

When God showed me in 1991 that I was first a daughter, then a bride, the bride part had no meaning beyond being someone's wife. I merely thought God was refounding the core of my identity as a daughter of God before anything else.

This was certainly true, but there's something sneaky about God's word to us. It has layers of meaning.

Perhaps you've experienced reading a Scripture verse you've heard 10 times before and all of a sudden it leaps off the page. The verse has new meaning because your life circumstances have changed.

It sounds really noble to say "forgive your enemies" or "nothing is impossible for God" until unforgiveness is hardening your heart or you're unable to conceive a child because of infertility. It's then that Scripture takes on new power and new authority, and sometimes we feel it's written just for us.

The same can be true of spiritual insights—words, phrases, or images we receive in prayer. For years, I focused exclusively on the daughter part of "first a daughter, then a bride." That is until the summer of 1997.

High Flying Romance

That summer I was flying high...literally. I'd met a man who danced Argentine tango and who lived 500 miles away in Massachusetts. Four out of five weekends I flew to Massachusetts to nurture this blossoming romance. And what a wonderful romance it was.

We went hiking, roller blading, sailing, and camping. We danced tango and sipped wine while sitting in his hot tub looking at the stars. I felt alive, free, and passionate again. I no longer felt as if I carried the burden of my life alone. I began dreaming of the possibility of a future together, and for the first time in years, I allowed my romantic love to be stirred up.

Then the plane crashed...figuratively. Just before I left for a three-week trip to Buenos Aires, Argentina, he broke the news: Although he loved me, he couldn't see a permanent future for us because of our religious differences. He thought it better to break off the relationship now rather than cause me more pain later.

More pain? My heart couldn't absorb the thought, it was already so numbed by pain. I cried. He cried. We both cried, and I got on the plane to go back to Ohio and endure the agony of a bleeding heart alone.

Redirecting the Heart

Over the next two months, I tried to be brave. I tried to get my heart to neutral, to convince myself of all the reasons why our relationship wouldn't work.

Instead, I kept discovering all the reasons why our relationship should continue. Now, all that was being wrenched away from me, and my heart was bleeding. I wanted to bandage my heart, to bind it up, to make it stop bleeding and take away the hurt.

Broken and Open

Then one morning I realized my heart wasn't just bleeding, it was broken. This man had broken my heart. It hurt so much to admit it. But in that moment of admitting it, the Holy Spirit showed me something else. He showed me Jesus too had a broken heart, and it was from his broken heart on the cross that God's love and mercy flowed.

God was asking me not to bind up my heart but to leave it open, to have a broken and open heart so God's love could flow from my heart to the world. So I began to pray, **"O Lord, make my heart broken and open."**

Aspirin or Microscope?

That prayer, however, didn't take away all the pain. I've discovered prayer isn't like an aspirin tablet that we take and, poof, a half-hour later the pain is gone. Prayer is more like a microscope that reveals more and more of what is unseen to the human eye.

Unpeeling the Layers

I kept praying and asking the Lord to reveal to me the source of my pain, and this is what he showed me:

Loss of a Love

Layer #1 was, of course, the loss of a love. It was difficult and painful to let a romance die. But there was more.

Loss of Hope

Layer #2 was the loss of hope. Like most women, I was guilty of having the future all planned out: We were going to spend Thanksgiving and Christmas together. I was planning to surprise him for his birthday; and I was even thinking of moving closer to him so we could spend more time together.

Now, suddenly, I was forced to re-image my future without him, and it seemed impossible. Who would I go roller blading, sailing, and dancing with? Who would hold me and kiss me and bring sunshine and laughter into my life? Who would help carry the burden of my life? I was struggling with a major loss of hope.

But the Lord didn't leave me in this state for long. In fact, the day after I realized I was suffering from a major loss of hope, a woman from Canada called and asked me to lead a retreat for 200 women a whole year later.

Just when I felt as if the lens of my world was closing in, the Lord was opening it up. He was using a wide-angle lens to help me see new possibilities and new opportunities for the future without this romance.

Slumbering Giant

Then there was layer #3, which was getting closer to the heart of the matter. All my desires for intimacy, companionship, and even marriage resurfaced. My romantic passions had been reawakened within me like a slumbering giant and had no where to go.

That's what hurt so much. This man had waltzed—well, he'd tangoed—into my life, stirred up my desires for intimacy and romance, and then left. And I was powerless to do anything. I was powerless to change him, powerless to make him love me, powerless to make someone else love me.

With this understanding the last layer peeled off, and I was left staring at the core of my pain: my deep need to belong.

Wanting to Belong

I thought I would belong to this man. I thought I would belong to his world, to the future we would build together, to the life we would share dancing, teaching tango, and raising a family. This was the deepest source of my pain—feeling as if I had no where to belong.

With this realization, God began a new work in me. He showed me I did belong to someone. I belong to Christ. I began telling myself a dozen times a day, "I belong to Christ. I belong to Christ." Sitting at my computer, driving the car, washing dishes, I kept repeating over and over, "I belong to Christ."

Not only that, I realized I belong to the Body of Christ. I belong to my dear friend Maureen in San Diego, to Donna in Buffalo, to Jane in Louisiana, to C.C. in New York. I belong to my son Michael, to the kids I teach confirmation, to the women in my faith sharing group. I even belong to you.

This was the beginning of living not just as a daughter, but as a bride.

Wider View of Love

When most people think of spousal love, they restrict it to the love between husband and wife. God, however, wants to open the lens of our minds and give us a wider view. He's inviting each of us not only to be a daughter of the Father, but to be a bride, the bride of the Spirit. He's inviting you into spousal union with himself.

Now you may be thinking, "Time out! I can handle being a daughter of the Father, but living in spousal union with God? You've got to be kidding! Isn't that just for saints and ultra-holy people?"

Yes, it is, but we're all called to holiness, we're all called to be saints. You can't check an "exempt" box on the form of life to opt out. Living in spousal union with God is for all of us.

Brain Freeze!

If you're in shock, I understand. Sometimes it takes a while for new and unfamiliar ideas to gain entrance to the castle of our minds. We see this pattern even in the gospels.

At the Last Supper, Jesus bent down to wash Peter's feet. Immediately, Peter put up a fight. The idea of a rabbi washing his disciples' feet was just too weird. It made Peter's brain lock up.

But Jesus didn't give up. He gently explained the purpose of his actions, and Peter jumped on board begging for an entire bath!

If you're feeling a bit like Peter and your brain is locking up, give your brain a rest. Let a spousal relationship with God remain on the other side of the moat for a while. When it doesn't seem so strange, let the drawbridge of your heart down, relax, and pick up this book again.

A Divine Date?

If you're only mildly in shock, you're probably wondering, "How do we enter into spousal union with God?" Do we e-mail him to make a date?

Let me share something that's a mystery to me. **The only way we enter into spousal union with God is through pain and suffering.** I know it sounds crazy, but it seems to be the way it works. And it works this way because God has to create in us more room for himself.

The Ultimate Housekeeper

Most of us live with lots of interior clutter. We have attachments, guilt, anger, and fear that take up interior space and crowd out God. It's kind of like spiritual cholesterol—it clogs up our interior life and reduces the flow of grace within us.

So what does God do? He undertakes some serious interior housecleaning to remove the interior clutter. But that's painful. It's painful to let go of the things we depend on for security, that give us pats on the back, that allow us to think we're in control.

In case you hadn't noticed, women have a huge need for security. As a result, we cling to things and people. We cling to our hopes for the future. We even cling to old wounds and patterns because they're familiar.

Preparing a Bridal Chamber

God knows this. He also knows that in order to espouse us to himself, he has to create in us more room for himself. He has to hollow us out.

This was the marvelous work I realized God was doing in me. Through the pain and loss, he was carving in me more room for himself. He was making a bridal chamber where only he could dwell.

Heart-Ache

How did I know this? Instead of ignoring the pain in my heart or trying to rise above it, I began using the pain as a constant invitation to conversation with God. While working, folding laundry, or going to sleep, I allowed the constant ache in my heart to remind me to talk to God, to pray.

As I did this, slowly the pain began to feel different. Instead of a gaping hole through which all my insides spilled out, the wound began to have a warmth, a presence. It became a divine wound that sparkled in my soul constantly reminding me of God's presence.

I understood God was espousing me to himself. He was making me his bride, and this was a diamond in my soul that was his betrothal ring to me.

More Intimacy

The thing that intrigues me about this whole experience is that I had nothing to do with it. If it had been up to me, I would have been married to my tango friend and dancing happily ever after. But that wasn't God's intention. Instead, he wanted to reawaken in me a desire for spousal love on the human level in order to create in me a deeper capacity for spousal love on the divine level.

Forgive me if I repeat that sentence: **God wanted to reawaken in me a desire for spousal love on the human level in order to create in me a deeper capacity for spousal love on the divine level.**

He wasn't allowing pain and suffering in my life just for the sake of pain and suffering. It had a purpose. My ache for human intimacy opened the drawbridge of my heart to the possibility of divine intimacy.

Shortly after this experience, I tried to capture the sovereignty of God's action through poetry. Here's what I wrote:

> *Diamond, diamond in my soul.*
> *How did you get there?*
> *If it was me,*
> *I would not know.*
>
> *But it is You, You are the Jeweler*
> *Who wounds with a gem of love.*
> *You make the mark so deep,*
> *Chiseled there by pain.*

How can a wound be one of love?
How can pain be that of deepening?

For You did not wait for my consent,
Nor hesitate, pending my approval.
The setting is ready; the diamond awaits.
The circumstances conspire their approval.

Now the breaking happens.
My heart is broken and open.
No mending, no binding,
Just broken and open for love.

You place the jewel within,
Its light flashing through the fog of my pain;
A constant reminder of your promise to me.
A constant reminder of your presence.

The diamond, the promise,
They find no origin in me.
They are symbols of your extravagant love,
A covenant wrought solely by the Jeweler's hand.

Ordinary Spousal Living

In response to this divine wound of love, I began telling the Lord I wished I could live as the spouse of the Spirit. Quite to my surprise, he showed me I already was.

I was thinking of spiritual espousal as some future reality, as something to do with mystical ecstasy. This may be true for some, but living as the spouse of the Spirit is much more concrete than that. It's living our daily lives in union with God.

When someone gets married, he or she is bonded to the other person and carries a sense of that bond wherever they go, whether it's to work, shopping, or golf.

The same is true of a spousal relationship with God. He goes with us wherever we go. It's impossible to separate who we are from our relationship with God. Even though we may not express our faith explicitly in everything we do, just like married people don't talk about their spouse in every conversation, still our faith is inseparable from who we are and what we do: We flip pancakes in union with God. We ride the subway in union with God. We take out the trash in union with God.

So please, even though it hurts, don't be afraid of the pain. It's the Divine Artist's tool to carve in you more room for himself, to prepare the bridal chamber.

A New Grace

Secondly, it's worth repeating that a spousal life isn't just for a select group of mystics and saints. Neither is it a communion of spirits that happens only when you get all your kids down for a nap at the same time, or lock yourself in the bathroom for 10 glorious minutes, or retire from work or mothering and enter the convent. It's a grace available in the here and now for everyone.

John Paul II repeatedly called for a new springtime and a new evangelization. The prophet Isaiah says of God, "See, I am doing something new! Now it springs forth, do you not perceive it?" (Is. 43:19).

Bridal Bootcamp

God is doing something new. Never in the history of the Church has God offered this bridal invitation in such a lavish manner to laity and religious alike. It's part of God's new springtime. It's our bridal boot camp for the new evangelization.

What a funny phrase—bridal bootcamp! (Doesn't it make you think of a bunch of soldiers running through an obstacle course in wedding gowns?) However, like military boot camp, God uses pain and suffering in our lives to condition us for the task ahead, to bring about greater detachment from our way of doing things and a greater freedom to respond to his invitations.

The new evangelization isn't a "same-old, same-old" presentation of the gospel. It's lay people like you and me entering into a bridal relationship with God himself. That's new. That will rock the world!

A Nuptial God

Besides the new availability of this spousal grace, there's another reason why a spousal life is for all of us: because God is spousal.

God is not just one. He's a union and communion of fruitful, self-giving love. God in his very being is nuptial. That means whenever God acts, it's always for the purpose of union.

If there's one thing I'd want you to take away from this book it's this: **God always acts for the purpose of union.** Put it over your sink. Tape it to the inside of the dryer door. Post it on your steering wheel. God always acts for the purpose of union.

All for Union

If today you're diagnosed with breast cancer or your teenage son is arrested by the police, God is acting for the purpose of union. If next week, your financial debt surpasses the height of Mt. Everest or you want to strangle your boss (or husband), God is acting for the purpose of union. If you feel you can't wake up one more day alone or depressed, God is acting for the purpose of union.

In the Old Testament, God constantly wooed Israel back to himself through tragedy, famine, and trial. He always acted for the purpose of union.

In the New Testament, St. Paul transposes this nuptial imagery to an entirely new level. In Ephesians 5, he writes: "'For this reason a man shall leave his father and mother, and shall cling to his wife, and the two shall be made into one.' This is a great foreshadowing [mystery]; I mean that it refers to Christ and the Church" (Eph. 5:31-32).

Marriage: The Great Mystery

I pondered this Scripture for years until finally it hit me: marriage is a "sneak preview" of the spousal union God wants to have with us. The "great mystery" is not only that husband and wife become one flesh, but we can become one with God in a way that surpasses marital union. We can become the spouse of the Spirit.

Listen to God's tender words spoken through the prophet Hosea: "I will espouse you to me forever: I will espouse you in right and in justice, in love and in mercy; I will espouse you in fidelity and you shall know the Lord" (Hos. 2:21-22).

The "great mystery" is that God wants to marry us! We not only have a universal vocation, a feminine vocation, and a unique vocation, we also have a "final" vocation, a vocation in heaven. Every woman's journey finds its consummation in this vocation. John Paul II speaks about this final (or eschatological) vocation when he reflects on Jesus' conversation with the Sadducees.

One Bride for Seven Brothers?

The Sadducees contrive a ridiculous scenario in which a woman successively marries seven brothers. Each one dies without leaving any children. In the resurrection of the dead, they want to know, whose wife will she be? The Sadducees are sure Jesus will either deny the resurrection of the dead or endorse a type of heavenly polygamy.

Jesus chooses a third alternative. He responds: "You are badly misled, because you fail to understand the Scriptures or the power of God. When people rise from the dead, they neither marry nor are given in marriage but live like angels in heaven" (Mk. 12: 24-25).

Married to God!

In heaven, we neither marry nor are given in marriage because we are espoused to God himself! The nuptial meaning of the body finds its ultimate fulfillment through spousal union with God in heaven. This is the reason we were created and saved— not just to be "safe" from the fires of hell, but to be nuptially united with God forever.

The last book of the Bible (Revelation) ends with the marriage celebration of Christ and the Church (Rev. 19:7 and Rev. 21:2, 9-10). This is the fulfillment of time and history. Time and history exist to reunite Christ and his Bride.

The Bride of Christ, however, is not just a biblical manner of speaking. We are the Bride. We are the Church. Each of us enters the jubilee door of heaven as a bride adorned for her wedding.

Heaven on Earth

Amazingly, we don't have to wait until heaven to experience our final vocation. Christ, our Bridegroom, has already given us his body and blood. He's already made a total, complete, and irrevocable gift of himself to us upon the cross. And he's left his total, complete, and irrevocable gift of himself to us in the Eucharist.

The Eucharist, as Dr. Scott Hahn loves to say, is our heaven on earth.[1] It's where time and eternity meet. When we receive Jesus' body and blood, we enter into one-flesh union with him. In those precious moments of Eucharistic communion, Bride and Bridegroom are so united as to be one flesh. We leave father, mother, spouse and children, to cling to our Bridegroom and become one body with him.

Banquet Table or Bridal Chamber?

This is not the language of symbol; it's the language of reality. If the Eucharist were only a symbol, Jesus would be inviting us to the banquet table, to come and sit next to him. But it's more than a symbol. The Eucharist *is* the body and blood of Christ. Jesus invites us to the bridal chamber, to one-flesh union with himself.

Jesus insisted in John 6 that he was speaking literally, not figuratively, about his body and blood. When the crowds questioned his literal language, he didn't say, "Oh no, you misunderstood me," as he did in other instances to Nicodemus (Jn. 3), the woman at the well (Jn. 4), and Lazarus' sister Martha (Jn. 11).

Instead, he said with even more authority: "Let me solemnly assure you, if you do not eat the flesh of the Son of Man and drink his blood, you have no life in you.... The man who feeds on my flesh and drinks my blood remains in me, and I in him" (Jn. 6:53, 56).

Jesus Completes His Mission

Jesus couldn't back down. It would betray his whole mission. The human race would remain unwed. The Father's plan from all eternity to enter into nuptial union with us would remain unfinished.

Instead on the cross Jesus declared, "It is finished." God's plan for mankind was consummated. Christopher West, an author and speaker on John Paul II's theology of the body, describes Jesus' gift of self this way: "Christ left his Father in heaven. He left the home of his mother on earth—to give up his body for his Bride, so that we might become 'one flesh' with him."[2]

The Greatest Gift

The Real Presence of Jesus in the Eucharist is the greatest gift God has ever given to mankind. It is the Gift of his very self to us. In the Eucharist, God gives himself to us not only spiritually, but physically as well.

This reveals the most profound truth about the human body. **The body is not only nuptial, but Eucharistic.** It's made for nuptial union between husband and wife *and* for one-flesh union between each person and Christ.

Communion Not Contraception

We shouldn't be surprised that as belief in and devotion to the Real Presence declines, sexual activity outside of marriage skyrockets. The two are related. The deepest yearning in our hearts is for nuptial union.

Consequently, when we fail to experience the Eucharist as nuptial union with Christ, we search for this union elsewhere. Instead of teaching our young people the finer points of contraceptive use, we should teach them how to live the Eucharistic life.

The Eucharistic life is the antidote to the sexual revolution. It reverses the "maximum pleasure/minimum effort" trend of the past forty years and returns us to a Love that suffers, a Love that lays down its life for another, a Love that is total, faithful, fruitful, and irrevocable.

Prolonging the Real Presence in the World

Igniting a Eucharistic revolution doesn't mean every person has to join a cloister and spend the rest of his or her life in perpetual Adoration. Rather, it means the union and communion we experience in the Eucharist becomes the reality out of which we live every moment of the day. Whether we're at work, home, or the football stadium, our words and actions should prolong Christ's Real Presence in the world. As single, married, or celibate Christians, our life should be one of fruitful, self-giving love.

12 Ways to Live the Spousal Life

Perhaps this sounds a bit abstract, so let's get concrete. How do we practically live this moment-by-moment union with God?

How can we jump into the spousal current on the fourth part of the journey? Here are 12 suggestions drawn from my own life. Please don't feel as if you have to implement them all at once. Let the Holy Spirit show you how to begin and how to proceed.

1) Be More — Do Less

So often we think we have to "do" more. The last thing I want to do is pile more on your already full plate. One of my hopes for this book has been to help you "be" more: Be more as a daughter of God; be more as a woman; be more as the unique person God created you to be. As you live more out of your being, I think you'll find you're driven to do less. After all, we're human beings, not human doings. You don't "do" a bride; you "are" a bride.

2) Discover "Prayer of the Moment"

Spend time with your Divine Spouse; this is what we call prayer. However, most people complain they don't have time to pray, so I'd like to share with you the secret of spousal prayer. It's called "prayer of the moment," and it goes like this: whatever is going on in the moment, I use it to prompt me to pray.

When I'm washing dishes, I pray: "Thank you Jesus that you wash away our sins." When I'm folding laundry, I pray: "Lord please fold me (or whoever's clothes I'm folding) in your love and mercy." When I open the door to walk out, I pray: "Jesus help me open the door of my heart to you." When I turn the key in the lock, I pray: "Jesus help me never lock the door of my heart to you."

When I introduced this idea to a confirmation class I was teaching, they really got into the spirit. Here are some of the prayers of the moment they came up with: Feeling the sun: "Lord help me feel the warmth of your look." Carrying a bookbag: "Jesus thank you that you carry my burdens." Chewing bubble gum: "Lord may I chew on your word." Driving in the car: "Jesus lead me in the right path." Doing math: "Help me to forgive others 70 x 7."

What I love about prayer of the moment is three things:

✟ We can never say we're too busy because it doesn't take extra time—it just takes being present to the present moment.

✟ We can teach our children how to pray this way and so prayer becomes part of their culture from an early age.

✟ It changes the way we react to circumstances in our lives. Instead of cursing a red light we can pray, "Thank you Jesus that I will never be late to heaven." Instead of getting angry over spilled milk we can say, "Thank you Jesus that you fill our cup to overflowing." This is one of the ways we can use the things around us and our circumstances to constantly bring us into union with God.

3) Get Your Senses Involved

Rediscover the rich, visual treasures of the Christian faith. Sacred art, statues, Advent wreaths, stations of the cross, different images of Our Lady, the Divine Mercy image, and Scripture verses placed around the house are visual ways to redirect our focus back to God. Before I sit down at my computer to work, sometimes I light a candle and ask the Lord to guide my work. The candle is a warm reminder of the Lord's presence beside me.

Maybe you could light a candle in the kitchen before you start dinner, or in the living room while you're cleaning house, or wherever you might be. Then every time you see the candle, allow it to bring you back into God's presence. (But please don't forget to blow it out!)

4) Get Your Hearing Involved

Get a small cassette or CD player, put it in whatever room you're in the most (make sure you have one in the car), and then use it. Play tapes of talks on spiritual subjects,[3] get the Bible on cassette or CD, and play Christian music. Sometimes we need something outside of us stimulating our minds and nourishing our thoughts about our Divine Spouse.

Often women complain their minds go to mush because they haven't had an adult conversation in weeks, or they're overwhelmed by the tasks they have to do, or they spend hours a day chauffeuring kids in the car or caring for an elderly parent. Use the time when your hands are busy but your mind is free to stimulate your thoughts about different aspects of the faith, listen to Scripture, and lead your spirit into worship.

5) Read the Lives of the Saints

If you don't have time to read the lives of the saints by yourself, then read to your kids, no matter what their ages. The most valuable present I received at Michael's birth was simple stories of the saints' lives. That's how I began learning about the saints. Then as my son grew, our stories became more sophisticated. You can read about the saints at the dinner table, bedtime, or family time. If you don't have children, read the biographies and writings of the saints and let them show you how to live a spousal life.

6) Celebrate the Lord's Day

Sunday is the wedding day of our soul. God doesn't celebrate his wedding anniversary to us once a year, but every week. Every

Sunday we're reminded that we are made for union and communion with God. When we rest from our work, it allows the nuptial meaning of the body to resurrect.

This means letting go of the things we want to *do* so we can *be* more: Invite others over for Sunday brunch (but make it simple so you don't end up cooking, doing dishes, and cleaning up instead of enjoying your family and friends); play soccer, go to the beach, or build snowmen as a family. If you're single, maybe you can volunteer for Big Brothers or Big Sisters, spend time in Eucharistic adoration, call a friend long distance, go bike riding, or have dinner with a family.

Except for rare occasions, I avoid doing laundry and housework on Sunday, and I try not to mow the lawn or go grocery shopping. I require my son to do his homework on Friday or Saturday and not wait until Sunday. This way it's really a day for him, God, and our friends. It takes discipline and planning to set aside the Lord's Day every week, but it's an invaluable way to nourish a spousal rhythm of life.

7) Make Time for Feminine Fellowship

Get together with other women to pray, laugh, cry, and blow off steam. As women, we need to develop close relationships with other women, to share our being with them, and to remind each other who we are in all our feminine fullness and originality. Meet with a small group of women two or three times a month, or commit yourself to calling someone on the phone once a week so as to keep in regular contact.

Ask your pastor about organizing a women's prayer breakfast, Lenten morning of reflection, or day of retreat. Remember, you don't just belong to Christ. You belong to the Body of Christ.

8) Read John Paul II's Writings

Start with John Paul II's "Letter to Women." Then read

"On the Dignity and Vocation of Women" (*Mulieris Dignitatem*) or "The Genius of Women." After that, consider reading "The Gospel of Life" (*Evangelium Vitae*), "A Call to Families" (*Familiaris Consortio*), or "The Lay Members of Christ's Faithful People" (*Christifideles Laici*).[4]

One of my goals has been to give you a primer in John Paul II's thought, kind of like his ABCs. Now when you read his writings, either on your own or in a group, hopefully you'll understand what he means by sincere gift of self, nuptial meaning of the body, and motherhood according to the Spirit. Then, allow the Holy Spirit to weave these concepts into your life and your vocabulary.

9) Ask God to Make You a Saint

My favorite theologian, Fr. Francis Martin, says a saint is someone in whom God works out the problem of the age. The problem of our age is precisely what we've been reflecting on in this book—what it means to be male and female.

Many Christian women are afraid of radical feminism because it redefines the human person and gender. Feminism, however, is pushing the Church forward in articulating her understanding of masculinity, femininity, and the body. Perhaps the Lord wants you to be part of this exciting development of doctrine. Give the Lord permission to work out in your life the problem of the age and let the Holy Spirit show you what it means to be daughter, woman, and bride in the context of your unique life.

10) Teach Your Sons How to Live a Spousal Life

Have you ever noticed how much easier it is for girls to be spiritual than boys? I saw this clearly when I was doing an hour of Eucharistic adoration and my neighbor brought her two girls, ages 8 and 10. They sweetly prayed for 45 minutes when my son (who was 11) wouldn't have lasted ten! We're doing a great job raising our girls to be godly women, but I ask you, whom are they going to marry?

This really concerns me. We need to teach our sons, grandsons, nephews, and godchildren how to live for union and communion through a sincere gift of self and not just for earning a living or to be a professional basketball player. (More about this topic in the next chapter.)

11) Cultivate the Eucharistic Life

Try to come into contact with the Real Presence of Jesus in the Eucharist more often than you do now. If you go to Mass once a week, try going twice. If you spend an hour in Eucharistic adoration once a week, stop in for 10 or 15 minutes another time during the week. If there's no Adoration near you, then pray before the tabernacle on your way to work or while the children are in school.

Matthew Kelly, an international speaker from Australia, says his time before the Blessed Sacrament is where he lets things float to the top of his heart and skims off what doesn't need to be there. That's a good model for all of us. Don't worry about what you're going to say. Just show up and let Jesus skim off your heart and life what doesn't need to be there.

The key to growing in the Eucharistic life is sustainability. Figure out what you can do over the long haul and then be faithful to it. And most of all, try to make a worthy reception of the Eucharist, to realize in the moment of receiving the Body and Blood of Christ, the Great Mystery is taking place in you. The two, you and God, are one. Don't rush your Eucharistic communion. Extend it as long as possible. Remember, this is your eternity.

12) Cultivate Your Relationship With Mary

The Blessed Mother is such a gift to us! Mary is the most perfect human example of the spousal life. She was the first one to fully live the Great Mystery, to live a bridal relationship with the Trinity. Mary's being and the Holy Spirit were so united as to be one. This is why she is called the Spouse of the Spirit.

God's Rainbow

Over the years, the Catholic Church's emphasis on Mary has been vigorously criticized. Isn't Jesus enough? Why do we need Mary? Doesn't she detract from Jesus' saving death?

Far from detracting from Jesus' life and death, Mary is the rainbow of God. Mary, like a rainbow, makes it possible to see what's usually hidden from view. Even though we know light is composed of a spectrum of colors, we see the fullness of this truth when a beautiful rainbow arches across the sky.

Likewise, even though we know Jesus' death upon the cross forgives sin and heals our relationship with God, we see the fullness of this truth when we gaze upon the beauty of Mary arching across history.

Everything the Church says about Mary flows from the cross and God's generosity. God paints the rainbow of Mary to make the abstract truths of the faith concrete for *us*.

Mary's Greatest Need

One Good Friday, I was preparing to venerate the cross when a new thought struck me: As Mary stood at the foot of the cross, she not only shed tears of sorrow, but tears of gratitude. She was witnessing *her* salvation. **Mary wasn't the one least in need of the cross. She was the one most in need of the cross**[5] because God applied the redemption of the cross to her *in advance*.

Saved From the Pit — In Advance

This idea of receiving the grace of the cross in advance seems odd to many people. However, there's an image I think helps. Suppose you're walking along a road and suddenly you fall into a 20 foot pit. Can you get out by yourself? No, you're condemned to die. But then someone comes along and pulls you out of the pit. Are you saved? Absolutely yes.

Now imagine you're walking along that same road and the person comes up to you in advance of the pit and takes you down a different path so you don't fall into the pit. Are you saved from the pit? Absolutely yes, *but in advance.*

This is the grace of the Immaculate Conception. Mary was saved from the pit of sin in advance through the cross of Christ. She received the grace of living in union with God, others, nature, and within herself between body and spirit from the moment of her conception. Her ability to live in union and communion was fully intact.

Immaculate Duct Tape

When I try to explain this idea to audiences, I often bring with me a piece of duct tape. A fresh piece of duct tape has its ability for union fully intact. If I stick it to something, it sticks and sticks well. But if I peel it off and stick it to something else, it sticks, but not as well. If I do that a dozen times, by the end, the duct tapes barely adheres. Its ability for union is compromised.

Because of sin in our lives, most of us are like that piece of duct tape. We stick ourselves to something or someone, peel ourselves off, stick ourselves somewhere else, etc. In the process, our ability for union becomes compromised. (Thank goodness for the sacrament of reconciliation, which restores our ability for union.)

Mortal sin doesn't mean someone is a horrible person. It means they've completely lost their ability for union through consciously chosen actions. It's impossible for them to "stick" to God.

Mary, on the other hand, is like immaculate duct tape. She adheres once and only once. Through her own free will, she preserved the purity of her ability for union and communion. She never sinned or broke her union with God. She never made a sincere gift of self to anyone or anything other than for God.

Making the Trinity Concrete

Mary is a precious gift to each Christian because Mary is an icon of the Trinity. In her, the entire mystery of the Trinity is enfleshed: The Holy Spirit espouses himself to Mary to conceive the Word of God in her, and lead all creation back to the Father. Mary is daughter of the Father, mother of the Savior, and bride of the Spirit.

As we say "yes," we become more and more like Mary. We enter more deeply into the self-giving mystery of the Trinity, and the Holy Spirit helps to heal the nuptial meaning of our body. Through our daily life in the Spirit, we gradually recover our ability to live in union and communion with God, with others, with nature, and within ourselves between body and spirit.

The Marian Way

As Christian women, we don't have to wonder where the current is taking us. Mary has illuminated the path before us:

✠ The Holy Spirit wants to espouse us to himself to conceive the Word of God in us and lead all creation back to the Father.

✠ Each of us is a daughter of the Father, mother of the Savior, and spouse of the Spirit.

✟ We are created to image God in our feminine
bodies, to bear Christ to the world, and to live
in moment-by-moment union with our Divine
Bridegroom even in the midst of pain and busyness.

Eucharistic, Trinitarian, Bridal, and Marian

Whether we are single, married, or celibate, our feminine
journey is truly one that is Eucharistic, Trinitarian, bridal, and
Marian. No wonder John Paul II believed that in Mary we
discover the true dignity of woman and that this discovery must
reach the heart of every woman and shape her vocation and life.[6]

May the third millennium find the imprint of Mary on every
woman's heart. Mary, Mother of the Third Millennium, pray
for us!

ЅꙄ

Questions for Reflection and Discussion

1. Have you ever thought of yourself as the spouse of
the Spirit?

2. What type of interior clutter takes up space within
you and prevents you from making more room for God?
Are you willing to give God permission to "clean house"?

3. What's your reaction to the statement: "God always
acts for the purpose of union"? What experiences in your
life confirm or challenge this belief?

4. Review the 12 suggestions for living a spousal life.
Which of them are you already living? Which ones could
you integrate into your life?

5. How do you pray now? Could "prayer of the moment" help enrich your relationship with your Divine Spouse? Compose three "prayers of the moment" based on activities you do every day.

6. Why is Mary so important to the life of the Church? How would you describe your relationship with Mary at this time in your life?

7. Write a prayer to Jesus telling him your thoughts and feelings about being His bride.

Chapter 7

ഒൽ

What About the Men?

funny thing happens after I speak about the dignity and vocation of women. I'm often surrounded by women anxiously asking: "What about the men?" I kept hoping John Paul II would let me off the hook by publishing an apostolic letter on the dignity and vocation of men, but he didn't.

Feminine Thoughts on Men

As a result, I've continued to pray, read John Paul II's writings, and talk to men about their life experience. Even though I'm not a man, I hope the following insights will be refreshingly original and spur men to reflect more deeply on their nature as men.

I also hope women will gain more patience and appreciation for the uniqueness of men and why God purposefully created us "male and female."

Back to the Beginning (Again!)

In order to understand the nature of men, we once again follow John Paul II back "to the beginning," back to creation and the fall in Genesis 2 and 3.

As I mentioned in chapter 2, John Paul II identified a deep and original unity between male and female. Women and men are not from different planets. They're from the same body. We are one nature, embodied in two ways, for the purpose of union and communion through a sincere gift of self.

This is what John Paul II called the nuptial meaning of the body, and it's the bottom line for understanding both masculine and feminine nature. (Forgive me for repeating myself. It's something I learned from John Paul II.)

In chapter 3, we saw woman's first presence in the world was as gift to the man. But now let's turn the scenario around and look at it from the male's perspective (with a little help from John Paul II).

Receiver of the Gift

If woman's first presence in the world is as gift, then the man is the one who, above all, receives the gift: "'From the beginning,' the woman is entrusted to his eyes, to his consciousness, to his sensitivity, to his heart."[1]

This is a beautiful image. Adam spontaneously opened his heart and life to Eve without hesitation or limitation. He didn't complain to God that she wasn't just like him, nor did he simply tolerate her presence. He accepted and loved her with all her feminine distinctiveness and uniqueness.[2]

Protecting Communion

Through accepting fully the gift of woman, the male discovered the nuptial meaning of his own body. He discovered that he, too, was made for a sincere gift of self, for a communion of persons and not just a solitary existence. John Paul II says it is the *man's* responsibility to protect this mutual self-giving because it's through *reciprocal* self-giving that a real communion of persons is formed.[3]

Gift vs. Appropriation

However, something happened to this communion of persons. It didn't stay reciprocal for long because Satan entered the picture. One of the most important concepts Genesis teaches is this: When God acts, he gifts. When Satan acts, he appropriates. He takes for his own purposes.

This is graphically dramatized in the garden. When God acted, he made all creation as a gift of his love. When Satan acted, he convinced Eve to take and appropriate the fruit for self-gain instead of self-giving.[4]

Where Was Adam?

But Eve is not the only one involved in original sin. There's an important and sometimes forgotten question that must be asked: Where was Adam? He must have been close by because Eve gave him the fruit to eat.

Yet the silence of Adam is deafening. He failed to intervene on Eve's behalf, to protect the communion of persons entrusted to him. He opted for mute passivity rather than self-donation. The original communion of persons shared by Adam and Eve with each other and God was shattered.

Competence Is King

Adam's failure to protect the original communion of persons is worth pondering. Dr. Larry Crabb, a Christian psychologist in the United States, has written an excellent book called *The Silence of Adam* in which he looks at why men fail to act.[5]

He says most men draw their worth and identity from feeling competent. Therefore, they live within the boundaries of their competency, investing time and energy in goals and achievements where they feel capable. This makes them feel like a man.

Confronted by Uncertainty

Life, however, is not always so neat or charitable. Men are confronted by unfamiliar territory where their adequacy remains unproven, their talents are useless, or they can't control the outcome.

When this happens, a sinister voice creeps in. It accuses them of being incompetent and unmanly. In response, men either become paralyzed by fear and retreat into passivity, or try to dominate the situation. In the story of original sin, we see both happening.

Sound the Retreat!

Adam first slips into passivity—he fails to intervene on Eve's behalf. He chooses to be silent rather than confront the relational chaos Satan is brewing.

Dr. Crabb says this pattern is repeated over and over again. Men retreat into their work, hobbies, or sports rather than entering into the relational sphere. They withdraw their gift of self from woman, leaving her to do the initiating and sometimes even the protecting.

The Fear Factor

Men do this out of fear, fear of entering the realm of mystery where the path before them is uncharted and they have to live in the unresolved. Every man I've ever spoken to tells me he hates to live in the unresolved. It's too messy. Most men dread watching another person (especially a woman) experience pain and suffering particularly if he feels helpless to do anything about it.

A Crying Woman

In our home, I'm always looking for opportunities to teach my son how to relate to women. One day, I plopped on the bed next to him and asked, "Michael, what do you do when a woman cries?"

He looked at me as if I'd finally gone off my rocker. Then he thought for a moment and said, "Hold her?"

"Yes! Yes!" I exulted, and gave him a big feminine hug.

Why do I torture my son with questions like this? Because when a man feels helpless, his basic instinct is to run and hide, to withdraw his gift of self because he doesn't think receiving and protecting her gift of self is enough. (It is enough!)

Independent Women/Absent Men

The outcome is resentful women and absent men. Women stop giving their gift of self to men and become independent women who don't need men, and men become confused about their identity because their competency is no longer valued or needed.

In short, when men fail to act, women develop an independency that excludes a real communion of persons. The result is isolation.

Domination Replaces Self-Donation

There's a second result of original sin, that of domination ("he will lord it over you..."). Original sin takes the communion of persons and twists it a different way. Instead of self-donation, there's domination. Men are tempted to regard women as a something instead of a someone.

In essence, domination reduces a woman from a person to an object. It zeroes in on the physical dimension and ignores the spiritual reality. A woman's body, and his as well, no longer have value because they are made in the image and likeness of God for a sincere gift of self, but because they provide the means for gratification, pleasure, and release, whether through intercourse, pornography, self-stimulation, or physical or emotional abuse.

Disposable Bodies

Unfortunately, Satan has done a masterful job of using our desires and passions to destroy the real communion of persons and the divine significance of the body. In the garden, the woman revealed to man the meaning of his existence: to exist with and for another, to make a sincere gift of self for *permanent* union and communion.

With original sin and the introduction of domination, the body is no longer treated as a gift but as a consumerist object. It can be appropriated and enjoyed for the moment and then disposed of without thinking of its divine image or value.

After original sin, the pendulum swings two ways: the male finds himself retreating from woman and the result is silence and isolation, or he appropriates woman and the result is power and domination.

The Third Way

Obviously there must be a third way, and this was the one I had been diligently pondering. The answer came to me in November 1998 when I was 31,000 feet in the air and had no where to go.

This is how it happened: I was flying back to the United States after speaking in Trinidad, West Indies, and I was enjoying the tranquil turquoise-blue water of the Bahamas below. I was also reading *They Call Her the Baroness*,[6] a biography of Catherine de Hueck Doherty, founder of Madonna House in Canada.

Priestly Desires

Catherine and her husband Eddie married later in life. Eventually, they decided to live a celibate marriage as a sign of solidarity with the single people who shared their ministry. As a result, Eddie felt called to the ordained priesthood, and he petitioned the Holy See twice for permission to become a priest. Twice he was denied.

One day a priest friend from the Melkite Rite, an eastern Catholic rite with married priests, visited Catherine and Eddie.

Eddie shared his struggle about priesthood. Their friend offhandedly replied if he was ever consecrated a bishop, he would ordain Eddie a priest. A week later, their friend was chosen to be a bishop.

At that moment, something broke inside me and I began to cry. I was quite surprised at my reaction since I identify more with Catherine than Eddie. Catherine was a writer, speaker, and single mother for many years like myself. Why would I be so moved that her 78-year-old husband received permission to be ordained a priest?

More Than a Husband

I composed myself and continued reading. Three paragraphs later, tears poured down my face. Eddie had returned to Madonna House after his ordination, and Catherine's first words to him were, "Your blessing, Father." **Eddie was no longer simply husband to Catherine, but priest.**

This was the answer I had been seeking for two years—that the nature of the male is not passivity or power but to be priest, to offer his body and blood for the sanctification of the world.

In my talks about the dignity and vocation of women, I explain how motherhood is knit into the very structure of a woman's being (see chapter 3). This means some women are called to biological motherhood, but *every* woman is called to spiritual motherhood.

Every Man's Call

At last I had the male counterpart: some men are called to ordained priesthood, but **every man, without exception, is called to spiritual priesthood because priesthood is knit into the very structure of a man's being**. He offers his body and blood so others can draw closer to God. His life is a sacrificial offering not for material comfort, status, or power, but to purify his family, wife, neighborhood, and workplace of sin and its effects.

That's a mighty tall order. It's also painfully countercultural in a society that has lost the distinctiveness of the ordained priesthood. While priesthood is certainly pastoral in nature, its essence is one of reparation, an offering of life for the forgiveness of sins.

Forgiveness Through Blood

The Old Testament abounds with this theme. During Passover, the Israelites spread lamb's blood on the doorposts as a sacrificial offering. A lamb had to give up its life for that offering.

On the Day of Atonement, the high priest entered the Holy of Holies and sprinkled the mercy seat of the ark with blood from an unblemished lamb as an act of purification from sin. A lamb had to give up its life for that purification.

In the New Testament, John the Baptist sees Jesus and cries out, "Look! There is the Lamb of God who takes away the sin of the world!" (Jn. 1:29). This statement would have sent a seismic shock through its hearers. John is declaring that Jesus of Nazareth will give up his life as an atonement for sin.

The Great High Priest

The book of Hebrews develops Jesus' priesthood more completely. Jesus, the great High Priest, offers not the blood of bulls and goats for the forgiveness of sins, but his own blood on the new mercy seat of the cross. Hebrews 9:22 makes this divine plan clear: "According to the law almost everything is purified by blood, and without the shedding of blood there is no forgiveness."

Jesus' total and complete gift of self to us on the cross purifies us of sins and its effects. He offers his body and blood on the cross for the sanctification of the world.

The Fatherhood Connection

Not only are sacrifice and sanctification painfully countercultural, but two other realities aggressively under attack today are motherhood and fatherhood. Abortion, contraception, embryonic stem cell research, and homosexuality deny motherhood and fatherhood.

Sadly, the Church isn't exempt. The current battle to remove masculine references to God in Scripture and the liturgy is a direct attack on the Fatherhood of God.

This attack on fatherhood affects the priesthood as well. We don't call a priest "Master" or "Teacher" but "Father." A priest is a spiritual father. Spiritual priesthood and spiritual fatherhood overlap.

Structural Design

Why? Because of the male body. In order to become a human father, a man has to give his body and blood, his semen, away. New human life will never be conceived if a man withholds his biological gift of self.

The same is true on the spiritual plane. New, spiritual life would never have been conceived if Jesus, the great High Priest, had withheld his gift of self, if he hadn't given his body and blood away.

Priesthood, like motherhood, is knit into the very structure of the body. Jesus *had* to be male. It was his masculine nature to give his body and blood away just as it is a woman's feminine nature to receive and nurture new life.

A Priestly Mission

Every man is called to this same mission—to imitate Jesus' priestly act upon the cross by offering his body and blood for the sanctification of the world. A man's discernment isn't whether or not he should be a priest, but *how* God is calling him to be a priest—as an ordained priest to the Church, as a married man to his domestic church, or as a single man to transform society and culture from within.

A Domestic Mission

If I was on a deserted island and could only have one chapter of Scripture, I'd be tempted to pick Ephesians 5. This chapter not only talks about the "Great Mystery" of Christ's nuptial love for the Church, but it also describes the priestly role of the husband. Listen to what St. Paul says:

> "Husbands, love your wives, as Christ loved the church. He gave himself up for her to make her holy, purifying her in the bath of water by the power of the word, to present to himself a glorious church, holy and immaculate, without stain or wrinkle or anything of that sort. Husbands should love their wives as they do their own bodies" (Eph. 5:25-28).

St. Paul fills this passage with priestly vocabulary: holy, purifying, immaculate, gave himself up, body.

When men drag their body and blood out of bed in the morning to pray and then lead their family in prayer, they're being priestly. When a man's body and blood goes to work for the twenty-second year in a row, he's being priestly. When his body and blood resists the temptation to look at pornography or be unfaithful to his wife (even if she's his *future* wife), he's being priestly.

Priesthood, even spiritual priesthood, is incarnational. It happens in the body, not in some ultra-spiritual realm.

Bodily Offering

Priesthood requires the offering of flesh and blood. That's why Hebrews 10:5 says of Christ: "Sacrifice and [sin] offering you did not desire, but a body you have prepared for me," for it is through the body that we make a gift of self to God and others. Christ is head of the Church in order to give his body up for her. A man is "head" of his wife not to stroke his own ego, but in order to give his body up for her.[7]

Keepers of the Eucharist

In addition to sacrifice and spiritual fatherhood, there's a third dimension to priesthood. This is captured in the title of Fr. William Schaefers' classic book, *Keepers of the Eucharist*.[8]

As priests, men are keepers of the Eucharist. They are entrusted with the body and blood of Christ. This entrustment is obvious for the ordained priest, but what about men who are spiritual priests?

This is where our earlier reflections on Genesis can help us. All men, whether single or married, are entrusted with woman, with her body and blood. She is their Eucharist. They help make the Eucharistic miracle happen in her life.

Divine Transformation

What is the Eucharistic miracle? The ordinary elements of bread and wine become the body and blood of Christ. This same miracle is meant to happen in each of us. God wants to take the ordinary elements of our body and blood and transform them into the body and blood of Christ.

Men help this happen in women. By receiving a woman's gift of self, affirming it and not trying to change it, men awaken and heal in her the divine image. They help heal the nuptial meaning of a woman's body so she can make a sincere gift of self in all her feminine distinctiveness and potential for motherhood. Men help women become the body and blood of Christ in the world.

John Paul II was very clear about this: "The acceptance of the woman by the man and the very way of accepting her, become, as it were, a first donation....The woman, 'rediscovers herself'...because of the way in which she has been received by the man."[9]

As keepers of the Eucharist and imitators of Christ, men have the special privilege of regarding women with the same reverence and tenderness as the Eucharist. When they hold her, they hold the body of Christ in their hands.

Reaching Her Full Potential

A man's affirmation of woman as a feminine mirror of the divine image is so important. Hidden within the feminine personality is the Trinity: Daughter of the Father, mother of the Savior, and bride of the Spirit. When men affirm women in all their feminine distinctiveness and potential for motherhood, the female personality takes flight.

Ask any woman how she feels when men give her attention and affirmation without seeking anything in return. First of all, she's flabbergasted. Secondly, she soars. She feels free and energized to stretch, take risks, and fully develop her gifts and talents.

According to John Paul II, Christ acts in the same way as bridegroom of the Church—He brings the Church to the fullness of her splendor, without spot or wrinkle.[10]

Seeds of Life

And that brings us to our final image, that of bridegroom. As spiritual priests, men are the bridegroom of the Church. They implant within the Church and the world the Word of Life.

A man's word and his presence are potent. They have the power to give life or take it away, to make God present in his family and workplace or deny his existence. Every man is either a fertile contributor to the culture of life or a sterile pawn in the culture of death.

Total Recall

The Hebrew word for "male" is *zakar*, and it means "the remembering one."[11] Men are called to pass on the living memory of God in the world. They are not called to remain silent and allow Satan to spin his web of relational chaos and division, but to be like the New Adam, Jesus Christ, and speak forth the truth of man and woman's relationship with each other and God.

As the "remembering one," men preach Christ's total gift of self on the cross with their lives and words. They "make present" this gift of self at home, in the workplace, on the soccer field, and in the locker room. Fathers, uncles, youth ministers, teachers, and confessors must remind young men what our culture has forgotten—that men are made for union and communion through a sincere and fruitful gift of self.

By his word and witness, a man proclaims to the world that God is not a harsh, distant, and punitive father, but a loving, merciful, intimate, and forgiving father. John Paul II tirelessly incarnated this "remembering" presence in the world. He was a living icon of God's unconditional Fatherhood and Jesus' total emptying of self. The world will not forget the spiritual priesthood and fatherhood of Pope John Paul II!

Here Comes the Bride!

Finally, as male, spiritual priest, keeper of the Eucharist, and disseminator of the Word, every man must be in living contact with God. By meditating on Jesus' relationship with the Father and gazing on the cross of Christ, men re-encounter the origin and source of their masculine identity. In particular, each man must receive the spousal love of God and experience himself as the bride of Christ.

Yes, you read it right: I said "bride of Christ." This last area is so squeamish for men! It's fairly easy for men to relate to God as Lord, brother, friend, master, shepherd, and savior, but as bride? You've got to be kidding. That's women's stuff.

No it isn't, and here's why (in the words of John Paul II): "In the Church every human being—male and female—is the 'Bride,' in that he or she accepts the gift of the love of Christ the Redeemer, and seeks to respond to it with the gift of his or her own person."[12]

Receiving the Bridegroom

To be bride means to receive the sincere gift of self of the bridegroom. Jesus Christ has given his body and blood to us as the Bridegroom. And so each of us is called to personally receive that gift as bride.

To really change the world, men only have to do one thing: become bride. They need to open themselves completely to Jesus' total gift of self and allow the Trinity to penetrate their being, not just their doing.

Set Free

As a man opens himself more fully to God, new things happen. He experiences release from addiction and the realignment of sexual desires and drives. He's set free from fear of failure and the nagging dread of growing old alone. He no longer competes for power or pride of place, but seeks ways to serve and encourage others. His body isn't a tool to get what he wants, but the very instrument of salvation for others.

A priestly man is a holy man. He stands behind the altar of his life and says to his wife, family, friends, and the world, "This is my body given up for you." Through this self-giving, men incarnate Christ the Bridegroom in the world.

Divine Model

I'm sure by now you've noticed God's ways aren't our ways. This is clearly one more example. In order for men to become bridegroom, they have to first become bride. They need to experience the healing and empowering love of God. Then men will understand from the inside out why Christ's divine love as Bridegroom is the model and pattern of all human love and men's love in particular.[13]

The Gift of Gender

What a wonderful gift it is to be male and female, bride and bridegroom! As men imitate their Divine Bridegroom by offering their body and blood for the sanctification of the world, laboring right beside them are the Christian women God has called to be spiritual mothers by nurturing the emotional, moral, cultural, and spiritual life of others.

Spiritual motherhood and spiritual priesthood go hand-in-hand: as men lay down their bodies and blood to purify and redeem the world, so women lay down their lives for union. The result is astonishing. The more we are purified, the more we can live in union with each other and God. And the more we live in union with each other and God, the more we want to be purified so as to deepen that union.

Discrimination—Not!

A gender-neutral society is a sad and confused society. Discrimination is an evil, but distinction is God's design. Distinction creates beauty, uniqueness, unrepeatability, and passion for our specific contribution. The distinctions in the Trinity between Father, Son, and Holy Spirit imply no inequality but allow for uniqueness of relationship and mission.

The same is true on earth. The distinctions between male and female, spiritual priesthood and spiritual motherhood, bride and bridegroom all complement and explain each other. They give us our unique relationship and mission.

Let us beg the Holy Spirit to stir up this vision of spiritual priesthood in all men. Let us ask the Lord to bless and purify men everywhere so they can live a priestly life by offering their body and blood for the sanctification of the world.

☙✖❧

Questions for Reflection and Discussion

1. Before reading this chapter, how would you have described the nature of the male?

2. In your relationships have you experienced passivity or domination resulting from original sin?

3. What is your reaction to the concept that spiritual priesthood is knit into the structure of a man's being?

4. If you are a man, how can you offer your body and blood for the sanctification of the world? If you're a woman, how can you help men develop their priestly charism?

5. What are your thoughts on men being "keepers of the Eucharist"?

6. What was your reaction to reading men have to first become bride?

7. Do you think men and women having different responsibilities and roles is discrimination or distinction?

8. Discuss how spiritual priesthood and spiritual motherhood go hand-in-hand.

ɛɔↄ၄

For Men

Consider the following 10 suggestions for stirring up your priestly identity:

1. Read the book of Hebrews.

2. Try to make one priestly (sacrificial) act a day.

3. Meditate on the Eucharist as a sacrifice sacrament, a communion sacrament, and a presence sacrament.

4. If you're married, pick an hour a week to watch the kids so your wife can spend the time in prayer or recreation.

5. Make a conscious effort to join yourself to the offering of the Eucharist at Mass.

6. Ask God everyday: "What does it mean to be priest to my wife, family, friends, and co-workers?"

7. Read an account of Jesus' passion and death and consider: What happened when Jesus died?

8. Read *The Silence of Adam* by Dr. Larry Crabb.

9. Read *The Impact of God* by Fr. Iain Matthew.

10. Read "On the Dignity and Vocation of Women" by John Paul II and meditate on how women teach us about love and self-gift.

Chapter 8

ഇ൪ര

Women Priests: Why Not?

I thought this book was complete until my mom read the manuscript. (Thanks mom!) Her one lingering question was, "What about women priests?" I had avoided one of the thorniest issues of our time, and being a good mother, she noticed.

The question of women priests deserves an answer filled with integrity. It isn't an easy answer nor a simple answer. In fact, there isn't just one answer, but three: the head answer, the heart answer, and the faith answer.

The Head Answer

The head answer looks at Jesus' words and actions in the Bible to try to understand his intentions.[1]

First and foremost, the Bible says Christ chose 12 men for his apostles. While this fact is indisputable, the question remains, "Why?" Why did Jesus choose only men? Was it because of the cultural customs of his time? Was he restricted to men because women priests would have paralyzed the infant Church before it even started to walk?

Not a Conformist

If we look at Jesus' other actions in the gospel, we clearly see he wasn't a conformist. Calling the Pharisees and Sadducees a "brood of vipers" and turning over the money changer's tables weren't exactly in line with Jewish customs. Jesus' interactions with women show a deliberate pattern of breaking Jewish and cultural norms. Here are a few examples:[2]

✝ Jesus talked publically with a Samaritan woman.

✝ He took no notice of the legal impurity that resulted from being touched by the woman with a hemorrhage.

✝ He allowed a woman sinner to wash his feet at the house of Simon the leper.

✝ He pardoned with compassion the woman caught in adultery and showed that women shouldn't be judged more harshly than men.

✝ He was accompanied by women in his ministry.

✝ Women were the first witnesses of the resurrection and charged with bringing that message to the apostles.

John Paul II described Christ's radical break with custom when he said: "*...in the eyes of his contemporaries, Christ became a promoter of women's true dignity* and of the *vocation* corresponding to this dignity. At times this caused wonder, surprise, often to the point of scandal...because this behavior differed from that of his contemporaries."[3]

Most Qualified
Equally important is Mary's presence among Jesus' followers

but not as one of the Twelve. If any one qualified for ordained ministry, it was she: sinless, docile to the Holy Spirit, and an intimate participant in God's plan of salvation. She had the inside track. She knew Jesus' mind and mission better than any one else.

Yet, as Pope Innocent III noted in the thirteenth century, "Although the Blessed Virgin surpassed in dignity and excellence all the Apostles, nevertheless, it was not to her but to them that the Lord entrusted the keys of the kingdom."[4] We can't gloss over this decision. We can't simply attribute it to cultural pressures. In fact, Jesus chose the Twelve according to the Father's plan after spending the night in prayer.

New Circumstances

After Jesus' ascension, the apostles brought the gospel into new situations and cultural circumstances. In Acts 1, Matthias was chosen to replace Judas Iscariot. Once again, Mary or any of the other women who had accompanied Jesus from the beginning of his ministry could have been considered, but weren't.[5]

Additionally, when Paul and others preached the gospel and established churches among the Greeks, the ordained ministers were likewise male. In this Greek milieu, women priestesses were common. Women's ordination would have been readily accepted.[6] This would have been the ideal time to extend Jesus' nonprejudicial view of women to include priestly ministry, but it wasn't. Why?

The Heart Answer

The head can only take us only so far in understanding Jesus' actions. It must be complemented by the heart answer. The heart answer looks beyond the data to penetrate the meaning or purpose of an action.

Beyond the Data

Let's take a quick example, a kiss. The head answer describes the data: two people meet, embrace, and one touches his lips to the other's cheek. But the heart answer asks: What is the meaning of this action or sign? Is it an expression of greeting, love, or betrayal? The heart answer tries to penetrate the visible expression of an action in order to grasp its invisible meaning.

In the Catholic Church, this dynamic of visible/invisible is encountered regularly in the sacraments. A sacrament expresses in a sensible manner something that is invisible and intangible.

The Matter Matters!

Priesthood is a sacrament. The priest represents Christ (the invisible reality) who acts through him (the visible reality). As early as the third century, St. Cyprian made this quite clear: "The priest truly acts in the place of Christ."[7]

A sacrament by its very nature has to be expressed through matter. **And it matters what the matter is!**

Water, not chocolate milk, is used for baptism because water conveys washing, cleansing, purifying—the washing away of sin. Bread is chosen for the Eucharist because it conveys nourishment and the many becoming one. Potato chips are not good matter for this sacrament because the one becomes many. Likewise, a man is chosen for priesthood because he is able to stand *in persona Christi*, in the person of Christ.

A Female Hamlet?

Does it really matter if a man portrays Christ? Can't a woman portray him as well? This would be similar to asking if it really matters if a man portrays Hamlet. Wouldn't it be the same if a woman acted the part?

Obviously not. Hamlet is a man. He acts, thinks, fights, and loves like a man. We can't substitute a woman for the role and pretend everything is the same.

The same is true of priesthood. We can't substitute a woman for the male Christ and act as if everything is the same.

Nuptial Vision

There's a second heart reason why the priest must be a man: he represents Christ the bridegroom who is espoused to his bride the Church.

The priest is not primarily an administrator, pastor, or preacher, but the bridegroom who offers his body and blood for his bride the Church.[8]

Gender Elimination

Unfortunately, we've lost this sense of nuptial imagery between Christ and the Church. If a woman offers the body and blood of Christ at the altar, the nuptial imagery is completely obscured. Bride is offering herself to bride. The bridegroom is eliminated. New spiritual life cannot be conceived.

In this view of priesthood, the distinction between men and women is irrelevant. A person of either gender is sufficient. We have become a Church of individuals rather than men and women who are bride and bridegroom.

Masculine Knitting

This leads to the third and last heart reason—the divine distinction between men and women. The dignity, vocation, and mission of men and women are not based on social roles but are woven into the very structure of the body. Every woman is called to spiritual motherhood because her body visibly expresses the maternal gift of self. Every man is called to spiritual priesthood because his body visibly expresses the priestly gift of self.

Only men can be priests because priesthood is knit into a man's nature to give his body and blood away. Only women can be mothers because motherhood is knit into a woman's nature to receive and nurture new life. One doesn't detract from the other. They bring freedom to the other to be what God has uniquely created them to be.

Soul Matters

At the heart of this vision of masculinity and femininity is the relationship between body and soul. As Christians, we believe the human person is a body/soul composite. The body and soul unite to form a single nature.[9] As a result, **there's no such thing as genderless human nature**. We always have masculine nature or feminine nature.

If, as John Paul II maintained, "the body is the expression of the spirit,"[10] then the souls of men and women are different. Souls and bodies can't be shuffled around like generic poker chips belonging to any player in any combination.

A gendered body expresses a gendered soul, and therefore something unique to the body/soul composite. That uniqueness is expressed in priesthood for men and motherhood for women. Priesthood and motherhood are the unique domain of masculine and feminine nature because masculine and feminine souls are different.

Power Play?

At this point, perhaps some readers still vehemently insist on priesthood for women as the only way to equality and power-sharing. I admit priesthood hasn't always been exercised as total self-giving service. In the past, women's participation in pastoral and administrative responsibilities within the Church have been restricted and even denied.

However, as we saw in chapter 3, John Paul II sought to change that. He asked the whole Church to foster feminine participation in its internal life in every way except for those sacramental tasks properly belonging to the priest. **Priesthood**

is not the last bastion of male superiority any more than motherhood is the last bastion of feminine superiority.[11]

In this chapter and the last, I've tried to show how priesthood is not about power but self-gift. Christ freely instituted a male priesthood not because of Jewish customs or cultural pressures, but because this choice represented a deeper reality—the male standing *in persona Christi* as bridegroom of the Church and an expression of the male's priestly nature.

There's still one answer left.

The Faith Answer

Ultimately, the male priesthood is a matter of faith. Christ revealed it that way, and we embrace it as an expression of Divine Revelation and not human logic. Other tenets of the faith fall into this mind-boggling category: the Trinity, the Incarnation, and the Real Presence in the Eucharist.

Beyond Logic

Human logic alone could never have deduced God as three persons in one. Who would have scripted the transcendent God being born in a stable with a fully human and divine nature? Who would have the gall to insist bread and wine could become the body and blood of God?

These are revealed doctrines of our faith that have been argued, maligned, denied, and misconstrued. The Montanists wanted to preserve the oneness of God so they dismissed Trinitarian communion. Arius denied the humanity of Christ and almost split the Church. The early Christians were accused of cannibalism while many modern Protestant churches regard the bread and wine as only symbols.

If we add the male priesthood to this list, I would say it's in very good company! Only when a cherished belief is threatened do we usually jump into the midst of it and try to understand it from God's point of view.

Pushing Theology Forward

The questioning of the male priesthood, just like the struggle with the Trinity, the Incarnation, and the Real Presence, can be fruitful. It can yield a fuller understanding of who God is in his nature and who we are in his image and likeness. It can also give us new language to speak about the mysteries of God while knowing full well that much remains veiled.

My prayer is that the head, heart, and faith of each Catholic would come to trust the teaching authority of the Church while seeking an ever deeper knowledge and understanding of the mysteries of the faith. The fruit of this trust will be vitally alive and authentically free men and women who make a passionate gift of their feminine and masculine selves to the world for the salvation of all.

❧❧❧

Questions for Reflection and Discussion

1. Before reading this chapter, what were your thoughts about women priests? Has your perspective changed?

2. Have you ever thought of Jesus as breaking the cultural norms of his time when relating to women?

3. Do you think it matters what the "matter" is in priesthood? Why or why not?

4. How does a woman offering the sacrifice of the Mass affect the nuptial imagery between Christ and the Church?

5. What areas in Church life would you like to see women more involved in? How can you help that happen?

Chapter 9

෨෮

Women in the Third Millennium: Our Dignity, Vocation, and Mission

*W*here there is no vision, the people perish," Proverbs 29:18 proclaims.[1] Today we might say, "Without a mission, women get depressed."

Emotional Roadkill

When women have no sense of mission, no sense of the journey's purpose, they're emotional roadkill—easily flattened on the pavement of life. The real tragedy for many women is feeling suction-cupped to an insignificant life. What they do is an unnoticeable blip on the global screen of life. How do we peel ourselves off this depressive pavement?

A New Power and Influence

A change in perspective always helps, especially when it's drawn from the wisdom of the Church. See if you can guess who wrote the following statement:

> "As you know, the Church is proud to have glorified and liberated woman...to have brought into relief her basic equality with man. But the hour is coming, in fact has come, when the vocation of woman is being achieved in its fullness, the hour in which

woman acquires in the world an influence, an effect, and a power never hitherto achieved. That is why, at this moment when the human race is undergoing so deep a transformation, women impregnated with the spirit of the gospel can do so much to aid mankind in not falling."[2]

This is an excerpt from the Second Vatican Council's closing statement to women. Written in 1965, it rings true today. Women have achieved an influence that surpasses previous times and ages.

A Varied Past

Until the mid-nineteenth century, women couldn't go to college or inherit property. Only in the twentieth century, were they allowed to vote and continue a professional career after marriage.

In the third millennium, women are CEOs, politicians, administrators, and business owners. They are doctors, lawyers, engineers, graphic artists, and teachers. Their presence is felt within the sphere of public life as well as the private sphere of the home. They are anything but insignificant.

At the same time, global society and culture are undergoing rapid changes that shake the foundations of human life. The memory of God is being rubbed out from schools, public places, and national constitutions. Economic systems are crumbling, and aggression and violence rip nations apart. For many women, advances in technology and medicine are elusive.

Open Wide the Doors to Christ!

But John Paul II, our witness to hope, never became discouraged. From the first moment of his pontificate, one theme trumpeted from his lips, "Be not afraid!"

His first papal homily on October 22, 1978, began with these words:

"Do not be afraid! Open, indeed, open wide the doors to Christ! Open to his saving power the confines of states, and systems political and economic, as well as the vast fields of culture, civilization, and development. Do not be afraid!"[3]

To open every door of human life to the person of Christ is the mission of women in the third millennium. Because women have acquired "an influence, effect, and power hitherto unachieved," she can open wide the door to Christ in settings and circumstances previously shielded from the gospel.

Guardians of the Future

The Council's statement also begged women to "watch carefully over the future of our race. Hold back the hand of man who, in a moment of folly, might attempt to destroy human civilization."[4] It reminded women that they are the first educators of their children, passing on to them the rich traditions of Word and sacrament.

A woman's mission today is the same as that of the first disciples: Be leaven in the world. Remake the fabric of culture and society into a Christian one. Transform the marketplace from within. Build a civilization of love. Be the Body of Christ on earth!

Root, Shoot, and Fruit

This mission, however, must flow from a woman's dignity and vocation. Without being properly rooted, she will be like seed sown in rocky soil, springing up for a time, but withering under the burden and toil of day-to-day life.

Embedding the Root

We can never begin with mission; it is the fruit. Instead, we must begin with the root—our dignity as daughters. This dignity embeds us in the nourishing heart of the Father and from there sends forth a shoot into the world, the feminine body. We must never forget that our vocation and mission in the world extends from our rootedness as daughters.

Sending Forth the Shoot

But the root is not the same as the shoot. The shoot extends forth and gives visible expression to what is hidden and unseen. The shoot of the feminine body encloses within it the special capacity for motherhood.

As the shoot matures, it sends forth the vines and leaves of spiritual motherhood, which entwine their presence into the moral, cultural, economic, political, and spiritual life of family and society. These bring into the public and private spheres a woman's capacity for self-giving, for seeing others with the heart, for valuing the dignity of each person, and for nurturing life.

Bearing the Fruit

The root and the shoot thus prepare the way for the fruit. They anchor and nourish a woman's dignity and identity so she is free to blossom. What is the fruit? It is her unique and unrepeatable presence in the world. It is a woman's passionate sense of having something to give at this time in history and her collaboration in the redemption of mankind.

In Full Blossom

A woman's being and personality fully blossom when she experiences within herself the cross and the Incarnation, when she bears Christ to the world while participating in the sufferings of Christ.

Through this interior marriage of the Incarnation and cross, she participates in the indwelling of the Trinity. She and the Father are united, and through their spousal life in the Holy Spirit, the fruits of faith, hope, and love mature in her in order to bear Christ to the world.

This, then, is a woman's unique and unrepeatable mission in the world. It is neither the root nor shoot, but the fruit of her dignity as a daughter and her vocation as a woman. It is part of the organic whole God made her to be. Her feminine identity flowers in the world.

More than Our Functions

As women in the third millennium, we must keep this multi-faceted vision before us. The pressures of work, mothering, cooking, and laundry constantly try to reduce us to our roles. They want to squeeze us into our functions and convince us that these are the mainstay of our worth and identity.

We must resist being reduced to our roles. We must resist being applauded for our doing while forgetting about our being. Women are more complicated than this. We are being and doing. We are unique individuals and mothers. We are interior and exterior. We are a co-existence of many opposites.

Our identity is a composite of our dignity, vocation, and mission. It is the root, shoot, and fruit all organically connected into one presence in the world.

Diamonds in the Light

This is the great vision of women the Catholic Church holds out before us. It's the vision that should give us peace, hope, and joy as we navigate the twists and turns of life. It should peel us off the pavement and set us free to walk upright, drawing emotional strength and courage from the truth of God's word pulsating within us.

The Church rejoices in having glorified and liberated women in her midst. These women are diamonds in the Light, radiating the true dignity, vocation, and mission of women in the world today. This is every woman's journey.

ജ◯ജ

Questions for Reflection and Discussion

1. What was your reaction to Vatican II's "Closing Message to Women"?

2. Do you feel glorified and liberated by the Church? Why or why not?

3. Does it help to image your dignity, vocation, and mission as a root, shoot, and fruit? Why or why not?

4. How can you make a difference in the Church and the world as a woman in the third millennium?

5. What are the most significant thoughts and ideas you've gained from this book?

6. How has your view of the "journey" changed by reading this book?

7. Write a prayer to the Holy Spirit asking for the grace to live your dignity, vocation, and mission as a woman in the third millennium.

End Notes

Chapter 1: First a Daughter, Then a Bride
1. Mary Reed Newland, *How to Raise Good Catholic Children* (Manchester: Sophia Institute Press, 2004. Original title: *We and Our Children*, 1954); *The Year and Our Children* (New York: P.J. Kenedy, 1956. Out of print.)

Chapter 2: Why Male and Female?
1. For a detailed review of ancient and medieval thinking on women, see Sr. Prudence Allen, RSM, *The Concept of Woman: The Aristotelian Revolution, 750 BC—1250 AD* (Grand Rapids: Wm. B Eerdmans Publishing Co., 1977) and *The Concept of Woman: The Early Humanist Reformation, 1250—1500 AD* (Grand Rapids: Wm. B Eerdmans Publishing Co., 2002).

2. John Paul II, *The Theology of the Body* (hereafter cited as *TOB*), (Boston: Pauline Books and Media, 1997).

3. *TOB*, General Audience of 11-7-79, p. 43.

4. *TOB*, General Audience of 11-14-79, p. 46.

5. Many people wonder why I include both union and communion in this description. Each word brings out a different nuance. Union often has a more physical connotation (the marital union of husband and wife) while communion implies interpersonal relationship (the communion of the Trinity). As human persons, we are created with the capacity for both bodily union and relational communion.

6. John Paul II, "On the Dignity and Vocation of Women" (Boston: Pauline Books and Media, 1988), no. 7.

7. My description of the Trinity is not meant to indicate a time sequence, as if the Father and Son existed before the Spirit. The self-giving of Father and Son and bursting forth of the Spirit are eternal.

8. See John Gray, *Men Are From Mars, Women Are From Venus* (New York: HarperCollins Publishers, Inc., 1992); *Mars and Venus in Love* (New York: HarperCollins Publishers, Inc., 1996); *Mars and Venus on a Date* (New York: HarperPerennial Publishers, Inc., 1997); *The Mars and Venus Diet and Exercise Solutions* (New York: St. Martin's Press, 2003).

Chapter 3: The Genius of Women

1. *TOB*, General Audience of 1-9-80, p. 60.

2. Ibid.

3. "On the Dignity and Vocation of Women," no. 18.

4. John Paul II, "Letter to Women" (Boston: Pauline Books and Media, 1995).

5. John Paul II, "The Gospel of Life" (Boston: Pauline Books and Media, 1995), no. 86.

6. See "On the Dignity and Vocation of Women," nos. 17-22.

7. John Paul II, "The Genius of Women" (Washington, DC: United States Catholic Bishops Conference, 1997), Angelus Reflection of 7-23-95.

8. See John Paul II, "World Day of Peace Message, 1-1-95, as included in "The Genius of Women."

9. "The Genius of Women," Angelus Reflection of 9-3-95.

10. Ibid.

11. John Paul II, "Welcome to Gertrude Mongella, Secretary General of the Fourth World Council on Women," May 1995, No. 8, as included in "The Genius of Women."

12. Ibid., no. 2.

13. See also John Paul II, *Familiaris Consortio* (Boston: Pauline Books and Media, 1981), Section no. 23 on "Women and Society."

14. "Letter to Women," no. 10.

Chapter 4: Sin and the Nuptial Meaning of the Body

1. *Catechism of the Catholic Church,* no. 376, describes our life of union (harmony) this way: "By the radiance of this grace [the grace of sharing in divine life] all dimensions of man's life were confirmed. As long as he remained in the divine intimacy, man would not have to suffer or die. The inner harmony of the person, the harmony between man and woman, and finally the harmony between the first couple and all creation, comprised the state called 'original justice.'"

2. *TOB*, General Audience of 4-30-80, p. 111.

3. Quoted from the New International Version of the Bible.

4. *TOB*, General Audience of 6-18-80, p. 121.

5. *TOB*, General Audience of 5-14-80, p. 113.

6. *TOB*, General Audience of 5-28-80, p. 115.

7. *TOB*, General Audience of 6-25-80, p. 123.

8. "On the Dignity and Vocation of Women," no. 10.

9. A wonderful book on the topic of feminine friendships is *The Friendships of Women* by Dee Brestin (Colorado Springs: Cook Communications Ministries, 2001).

10. *TOB*, General Audience of 9-17-80, p. 149.

11. *TOB*, General Audience of 7-23-80, p. 125.

Chapter 5: Weaving a Tapestry of Life

1. See *The Collected Works of Edith Stein, Volume 2,* "Essays on Woman," translated by Freda Mary Oben, PhD (Washington, DC: ICS Publication, 1987).

2. *TOB*, General Audience of 12-9-81, p. 242.

3. Fr. Marie-Dominique Philippe, OP, *The Morning Star* (Peoria: Congregation of Saint John, 1989), p. 254.

4. *TOB*, General Audience of 3-24-82, p. 268.

5. St. Symeon the New Theologian as quoted in "The Consecrated Life," John Paul II (Boston: Pauline Books and Media, 1996), no. 20.

Chapter 6: The Spouse of the Spirit

1. Scott Hahn, *The Lamb's Supper* (New York: Doubleday, 1999).

2. Christopher West, *Good News About Sex & Marriage: Answers to Your Honest Questions about Catholic Teaching* (Ann Arbor: Servant Publications, 2000), p. 21.

3. St. Joseph Communications (www.saintjoe.com or 800-526-2151) is an excellent resource for tapes and CDs about the Catholic faith. Also, Our Father's Will Communications (www.theologyofthebody.net or 866-333-OFWC) carries Katrina's talks and retreats on tape and CD along with numerous resources on the theology of the body and other topics.

4. All these publications are available from Pauline Books and Media (www.pauline.org) except for "The Genius of Women," which is available from the United States Bishop's Conference (Washington, DC).

5. The thirteenth century Franciscan theologian Bl. John Duns Scotus speaks of Mary's great need in his *Ordinatio* IIII, d. 3, q. 1.

6. See "On the Dignity and Vocation of Women," no. 11.

Chapter 7: What About the Men?

1. *TOB*, General Audience of 2-6-80, p. 71.

2. See "On the Dignity and Vocation of Women," no. 14.

3. See *TOB*, General Audience of 2-6-80, p. 71.

4. See *TOB*, General Audience of 7-23-80, p. 127, where, in speaking about lust, John Paul II says, "The relationship of the gift is changed into the relationship of appropriation."

5. Larry Crabb, *The Silence of Adam* (Grand Rapids: Zondervan Publishing House, 1995).

6. Lorene Hanley Duquin, *They Call Her the Baronness* (Stanton Island: Alba House, 1995).

7. Cf. "On the Dignity and Vocation of Women," no. 24.

8. William Henry Schaefers, *Keepers of the Eucharist* (Milwaukee: The Bruce Publishing Company, 1946. Out of print.)

9. *TOB*, General Audience of 2-6-80, p. 71.

10. See "On the Dignity and Vocation of Women," no. 24.

11. Crabb, *The Silence of Adam*, p. 79.

12. "On the Dignity and Vocation of Women, no. 25.

13. Ibid.

Chapter 8: Women Priests—Why Not?

1. For a detailed explanation of the Roman Catholic Church's teaching on women and the ordained priesthood, see the Sacred Congregation for the Doctrine of the Faith, "On the Question of the Admission of Women to the Ministerial Priesthood" (*Inter Insigniores*) (Boston: Pauline Books and Media, 1976) and John Paul II, "On Reserving Priestly Ordination to Men Alone" (Boston: Pauline Books and Media, 1994).

2. See "On the Question of the Admission of Women to the Ministerial Priesthood," nos. 10-11.

3. "On the Dignity and Vocation of Women," no. 12.

4. As quoted in "On the Question of the Admission of Women to the Ministerial Priesthood," no. 11.

5. See "On the Question of the Admission of Women to the Ministerial Priesthood," no. 11.

6. "On the Question of the Admission of Women to the Ministerial Priesthood," no. 15.

7. As quoted in "On the Question of the Admission of Women to the Ministerial Priesthood," no. 25.

8. John Paul II says, *"The Eucharist...is the Sacrament of the Bridegroom and of the Bride."* ("On the Dignity and Vocation of Women," no. 26)

9. See *Catechism of the Catholic Church*, no. 365.

10. *TOB*, General Audience of 7-23-80, p. 125.

11. The Catholic Church makes a distinction between the ordained priesthood and the baptismal priesthood. Every Christian by means of baptism is baptized into Christ's mission as priest, prophet, and king. Women share in this baptismal priesthood and therefore are called to offer their bodies as a living sacrifice (see Romans 12:1) just as men are called to be nurturing. However, because of Divine Revelation, which is also revealed through the structure of the body, the dominant charism in women is (spiritual and biological) motherhood and in men is (spiritual and ordained) priesthood.

Chapter 9: Women in the Third Millennium: Our Dignity, Vocation, and Mission

1. Quoted from the King James Version of the Bible.

2. The Documents of Vatican II, "Closing Message to Women" (Chicago: Follett Publishing Company, 1966), Walter M. Abbott, SJ, editor; Very Rev. Msgr. Joseph Gallagher, translator.

3. John Paul II's first papal homily (Oct. 22, 1978: AAS 79 [1978], 947).

4. The Documents of Vatican II, "Closing Message to Women" (Chicago: Follett Publishing Company, 1966), Walter M. Abbott, SJ, editor; Very Rev. Msgr. Joseph Gallagher, translator.

Post Script
ℰℛℂℛ

*O*n April 2, 2005, as I was speaking to a Byzantine Catholic audience on theology of the body and the Eucharist, Pope John Paul II passed into eternity. As the bells tolled and we paused in quiet prayer, a thought flashed across my inner being, "Now my life begins."

Everything in my life (and in this book!) had simply been a preparation for this moment—for continuing the legacy of John Paul II. Almost without my consent, the current was rushing around another bend. And yet for 13 years God had been channeling the current in this direction.

On June 16, 1992, I met Pope John Paul II. It was two days before my son's fifth birthday, and we had requested to attend the pope's private morning Mass (in Rome) as a special birthday blessing.

Our request was granted, and after Mass, we found ourselves in a large audience hall outside his private chapel. As John Paul II shuffled to greet each collection of visitors, he was visibly pained. However, his face lit up whenever a child or baby was in the group.

Our turn quickly arrived, and John Paul II handed each of us a papal Rosary. In return, my son handed him a small book,

The Titles of Mary. Delighted, he bent down, embraced my son, and kissed him. Then he placed his hand on my forehead and blessed me.

It was a blessing I will never forget. The vicar of Christ imparted a portion of his spirit to me. Next to the birth of my son, it was the most beautiful moment of my life.

In my spirit, I sensed I received new graces for motherhood. These graces were indeed for motherhood, but not biological motherhood. They were for spiritual motherhood.

At the time, I didn't even know such a thing existed—that I, as a single, lay woman could be a spiritual mother. I was still navigating the turbulent waters of my annulled marriage. But God was already charting a new course and infusing my being with the grace I would need. He was also introducing me to my spiritual father, John Paul II, who would guide me through the process of discovering the full truth about my feminine identity and the meaning and purpose of the body.

Thirteen years later, "Now my life begins." With the passing of John Paul II, it is with great joy and humility that I feel commissioned to lead others to the spiritual fatherhood of John Paul II and to ask for a portion of his spirit to rest on them. *Totus Tuus.* (Completely Yours.) Amen!

Talks, retreats, and workshops
offered by Katrina J. Zeno

Many of Katrina's talks and retreats are available on CD, video, and DVD from Our Father's Will Communications (www.theologyofthebody.net, or 1-866-333-0FWC). For more information about Katrina's speaking, to check her calendar, or arrange for her to speak in your area, please visit our web site at www.wttm.org or call 480-720-5715.

One-Day or Weekend Retreats:
"The Genius of Woman: Our Dignity, Vocation, and Mission"
"Going Deeper Into Prayer and the Eucharist"
"A New Look at Marriage, Sex, and the Eucharist"
"Mary and the Eucharistic Life"
"The Single Life: Mistake or Mission?"
"In the Divine Image: An In-Depth Walk Through John Paul II's Theology of the Body"
"Evangelizing the Culture"
"Turning the Titanic: Training Your Children in Chastity"
"Fixing Our Eyes on Jesus" (parish mission)
"The Role of Women in the Church and Society"
"Real Men, Real Life—A New Look at Sex, Love, and Women"
"A New Way to Be Human"

One-Hour Talks
"An Overview of John Paul II's Theology of the Body"
"Living the Eucharistic Pattern"
"Eucharist: Sacrament of the Bridegroom and the Bride"
"The Eucharist: Jesus' Total Gift of Self"
"Mary and the Eucharistic Life"
"The Mystery of Woman: A Garden Enclosed"
"The New Feminism" or "The Genius of Woman"

"The Role of Women in the Third Millennium"
"Feminine, Single, and In Love With Life"
"The Splendor of Man"
"The Gift of Woman"
"Women Priests: Why Not?"
"The Beauty of a Woman: Beyond Britney and the Bachelor"
"Sacred Beauty" (on modesty)
"Marriage: The Great Mystery"
"Theology of the Body and Charismatic Renewal: What's the Spirit Got to Do With It?"
"When God Changes the Script"
"The Way of the Cross"
"Chastity Formation for Teens" (for parents)
"St. Edith Stein: Hope and Promise for Our Time"
"Mary and Theology of the Body"
"The Single Life: Pickle Juice or Champagne?"
"Dating, Romance, and God: Recipe for Disaster or Success?"
"Who's Driving Your Car?" (junior high)
"This is *My* Body" (high school/college)
"Passing on the Faith—Basketball Style" (all ages)
"Teaching Children to Pray the Mass"
"Three to Tango"

⁖⁗

**To order this book, please contact
Women of the Third Millennium
(www.wttm.org)
or Our Father's Will Communications
(www.theologyofthebody.net)
(866-333-OFWC, toll free)**